hrac

Hal Hartley |

D1606239

Contemporary Film Directors

Edited by James Naremore

The Contemporary Film Directors series provides concise, well-written introductions to directors from around the world and from every level of the film industry. Its chief aims are to broaden our awareness of important artists, to give serious critical attention to their work, and to illustrate the variety and vitality of contemporary cinema. Contributors to the series include an array of internationally respected critics and academics. Each volume contains an incisive critical commentary, an informative interview with the director, and a detailed filmography.

A list of books in the series appears at the end of this book.

Hal Hartley |

Mark L. Berrettini

UNIVERSITY OF ILLINOIS PRESS
URBANA, CHICAGO, AND SPRINGFIELD

Frontispiece: Hal Hartley, courtesy of Zero Fiction Film /
the Kobal Collection.

Library of Congress Cataloging-in-Publication Data
Berrettini, Mark L., 1972–
Hal Hartley / Mark L. Berrettini.
p.   cm. — (Contemporary film directors)
Includes bibliographical references and index.
Includes filmography.
ISBN-13: 978-0-252-03595-1 (hardcover : alk. paper)
ISBN-10: 0-252-03595-X (hardcover : alk. paper)
ISBN-13: 978-0-252-07791-3 (pbk. : alk. paper)
ISBN-10: 0-252-07791-1 (pbk. : alk. paper)
1. Hartley, Hal, 1959—Criticism and interpretation. I. Title.
PN1998.3.H3695B48   2011
791.4302'33092—dc22 [B]   2010040214

For Margaret Walsh

Contents |

My thanks to James Naremore, Joan Catapano, the anonymous readers, and the staff of the University of Illinois Press for their guidance at all stages of this project. Thanks to Hal Hartley, Moritz Wessendorff, Josh Yumibe, John Esther, Dan Short, Susan Gerhard, Ron Magliozzi, Pilar Mayora, Sanam Madjedi, the staff of the Kobal Collection, and the University of California Press. I sincerely appreciate Robert Avila's permission to reprint his interview with Hal Hartley.

Thanks to Brenda Cozzens, to the library staffs at the University of Northern Colorado and at Portland State University, and to my students, who have offered me many insights in our conversations. Thanks to my colleagues at Portland State University, especially to the members of the Department of Theater Arts, Bruce Keller, Jonah Ross, and Katie Sinback. Many thanks to those who have helped to shape this book and other projects: Brad Benz, Tom Bredehoft, Eric Brunick, Joseph Chaves, Clark Farmer, Julianne and Michael Freeman, Randall Halle, Rita Jones, Erin Jordan, Ann Little, Brian Luskey, John Michael, M. J. Moseley, Jennifer Peterson, David Rodowick, Joe Schaub, Diane Waldman, and Sharon Willis.

I am grateful to Lisa and John Zimmerman, Simon Barker, and my consiglieres Kelly Hankin and Michael Kramp for their wise counsel, good humor, and comments about this book. I am fortunate to have a supportive extended family, and my thanks especially to Maureen Cramer, Caroline Berrettini, and Paul and Katie Berrettini. My parents, Jane and Paul Berrettini, give me endless encouragement and inspiration, and it is with much love and appreciation that I thank them. Finally, I have asked Marcelle Heath to read portions of this book far too many times, but she always aided me without complaint. She offers me astute criticism, enthusiastic advice, and much more. Her support is vital, and she has my unending gratitude and love.

Efficiency, Estrangement, and Antirealism

The Films of Hal Hartley

Introduction

Since the early 1980s, Hal Hartley has written, directed, and produced more than twenty short and feature-length films, several music videos, dramatic work for the stage, and operatic collaborations. Along with his unconventionally romantic plots and his deadpan, absurdist-comedic approach, a compelling thread within Hartley's oeuvre is his hyper-efficient depiction of narratives about transformation and actual and figurative escape. From attempts to escape one's past and familial and social expectations in *The Unbelievable Truth* (1989) to the global tumult and the reevaluation of established identities in *Fay Grim* (2006), Hartley's characters are in flux. They want to change their lives or believe that they must change; to challenge specious gendered and sexualized boundaries; to flee judicial or institutional authority; to break off romantic attachments or quickly form new romantic couplings; to set out to live in new locations or to live in new ways within old locales; and to collaborate with or compete against others to create distinct forms of aesthetic self-expression.

At the same time, Hartley has enacted his own escape—or, perhaps more precisely, breakaway—from the dominant modes of narrative cinema to rework standards of character development, story construction, cinematography, and mise-en-scène. Named "the Jean-Luc Godard of Long Island" in Peter de Jonge's 1996 *New York Times Magazine* profile, Hartley's films, like Godard's, attempt to disrupt habitual film viewing, pleasantly disorient us, and stimulate an active, even cerebral sort of spectatorship. As de Jonge writes, "Asked if he wants his audience to enjoy his movies, [Hartley] says: 'Enjoy? No, they have to work. Anything worthwhile necessitates work'" (20). Hartley describes his film-production process as "doing damage" to cinematic convention and "preconceptions" about film in his increasingly minimalist narrative films (Fuller, "Finding the Essential," ix; Fuller, "Being an Amateur," xxii). As Hartley attempts to break away from an unsophisticated model of spectatorship as consumption, his films address us as "cocreators" of meaning in which the relationship between viewer and filmic text is not static, one-way, or basic. All narrative cinema compels us to create meaning—we must make links between shots, infer story elements that are not shown, and so on—but Hartley's aesthetic and narrative choices do not fit neatly into the seamless structure of standard narrative cinema. Instead, his films are situated within a framework that draws upon efficiency and antirealism, a framework that is the most clear link between his work and Godard's.[1]

Critiques of realism such as those advanced by Colin MacCabe and Fredric Jameson (both of whom have written about Godard) provide an informative background for what I want to identify as Hartley's style of antirealist filmmaking. MacCabe uses the nineteenth-century realist novel to delineate what he names "the classic realist text" and its presentation of narrative discourse as reality ("Realism and the Cinema," 34). MacCabe writes, "Whereas other discourses within the text are considered as material which are open to re-interpretation, the narrative discourse simply allows reality to appear and denies its own status as articulation. [The narrative discourse] is taken up in the cinema by the narration of events. . . . The camera shows us what happens—it tells the truth against which we can measure the discourses" (36–37). The classic realist text is the form of film and television that dominates today, a type of filmmaking that has become synonymous with "Hollywood," "commercial," and "mainstream," even though, as MacCabe rightly notes, this dominance was not and is not inevitable ("Theory and Film," 58–59).

MacCabe and Jameson are concerned with the political and ideological ramifications of realism, since it helps maintain dominant and oppressive structures through the representation of reality *as* static, natural, and not open to interrogation or to reevaluation. Jameson and MacCabe draw on Bertolt Brecht's formulations of the Verfremdungseffekt, or "V-effect," which Jameson translates as "estrangement," "in keeping with its Russian ancestor (*ostranenia*—a 'making strange')" (*Brecht and Method*, 85–86 n.13). According to Jameson, the Verfremdungseffekt serves "to make something look strange, to make us look at it with new eyes, . . . or [as] a habit which prevents us from really looking at things. . . . [E]strangement unveils [appearances as] made or constructed by human beings, and thus able to be changed by them as well, or replaced altogether" (*Brecht and Method*, 39–40).

Hartley has mentioned Brecht in relation to his filmmaking, and while I do not think that he has the same political-ideological challenges in mind that Brecht, MacCabe, or Jameson do, he draws upon estrangement precisely as Jameson describes it: as a way to look differently and as a way to suggest change. Hartley's style of antirealism and his use of estrangement attempt to reveal the *construction* of reality within narrative films, whereby the goal of cinematic conventions is to "look and feel like" reality.[2]

Hartley's deployment of antirealism initiates an extreme in-mediasres element that plays out in the opening moments of virtually every one of his films, where we are shown actions without much context. Hartley has explained his avoidance of establishing shots in interviews throughout his career (see Fuller, "Finding the Essential," ix; Fuller, "Responding to Nature," ix). The contradictory feeling of such scenes is that we have missed *something*—having arrived at the theater too late?—while we also recognize that the opening credits are a supposed guarantor of having not missed *anything*. A similar disoriented feeling sometimes occurs within the films of Jim Jarmusch, a filmmaker to whom Hartley has been compared. Juan A. Suárez tells us that Jarmusch has described his own films in terms of spectators "'dropping in on'" characters "without ever feeling in full command of their stories or completely understanding their lives [because Jarmusch's] characters are only partly known: their circumstances and motivations are incompletely rendered" (4).[3]

A similarly disarming aspect of Hartley's films is their comic, quirky, absurd tone. Characters frequently faint, fall, or collapse in humorous displays, often without identifiable cause, and when Hartley depicts physical violence, it is slapstick, overdone, or even clumsy in its style. With all of the characters falling, it is hard not to imagine that Hartley's interest in transformation links to the Christian New Testament story of St. Paul, struck down and life-altered, although for Hartley's characters, transformation usually is not religious in nature.[4]

Hartley's characters become stuck in dialogue loops and circular conversations that are not meant to be "natural" but instead highlight the sometimes amusing problematic of communication—people do not listen to each other, are not swayed from their opinions or from their desires, or talk past each other. The veneer of fiction explodes as Hartley's characters say exactly what they think and feel, often in terms that are painful to each other, yet the actors infrequently move beyond mild melodramatic style in their delivery or blocking. This disjuncture between restrained or minimalist performance and the brutal honesty of the dialogue is humorous and challenges much of narrative cinema's fidelity to realist, naturalistic speech and to the enactment of emotion as a performance to be displayed.

Extended close readings of seven of Hartley's feature-length films follow. We will see that efficiency, estrangement, and antirealism allow Hartley to chart the struggles of individuals against the ideological precepts that pertain to public and private behavior, responsible actions, "common sense," and the cinematic conventions that support such ideologies (e.g., romantic characters who will live "happily ever after"). Quite often these conflicts are related to the restrictions posed by gender norms and are depicted as conflicts with authority figures—fathers, mothers, nuns, priests, sheriffs, CIA agents, judges, and politicians (see Fuller, "Finding the Essential," xxiii). Hartley's male protagonists struggle to live up to popular ideals of heteronormative masculinity, control, and violent mastery of the world around them, while his central female characters break from heteronormative conceptions of women as mothers, caregivers, and/or sexual objects.

Biography

This biographical sketch draws upon material that is included in interviews, reviews, and essays about Hartley's work, and in an earlier version of his official Web site, possiblefilms.com, when it included portions of interviews that were published later as Hartley and Kaleta's *True Fiction Pictures and Possible Films*, as *Kino prawdziwej fikcji i filmy potencjalne* in Polish, and as a part of Sergi Sánchez's *Las variaciones Hartley* in Spanish.

Born in 1959 in New York City, Hartley was raised in Lindenhurst, on Long Island. Hartley's mother died when he was eleven years old, and his father was a well-known ironworker who ran a construction crew in New York (see de Jonge 20). He graduated from Lindenhurst High School in 1977, briefly attended the Massachusetts College of Art, and later completed his undergraduate work at Purchase College, State University of New York, in the Conservatory of Theatre Arts and Film, graduating in 1984. Hartley settled in New York City after graduation and began to work for Jerome Brownstein's Action Productions, which made commercials and public-service announcements. Brownstein became one of Hartley's earliest producers, funded much of *The Unbelievable Truth*, and continued to work with Hartley throughout much of his career.

Purchase was foundational for Hartley, as noted in Michael Atkinson's "Purchase Power":

> What's the deal with Purchase, anyway? Hartley, stumping for his alma mater, maintains that it's a simple matter of art over commerce: "When I was there, between 1980 and 1984, the faculty saw the school not as a career training ground but as an art school. The program was allowed to be fairly elitist, and it had a high attrition rate. There wasn't a big emphasis on turning us into viable commodities. But a big part of what went into the 'Purchase Mafia' is that they made us do everything—you had to shoot film, cut film, record sound, everything. It's just like if we were art students, we'd be made to stretch our own canvases." The faculty at the time (which was when nearly all of the college's famous

grads attended) was led by '70s drop-out Aram Avakian and vet doc maker Willard Van Dyke, and consisted largely of working pros. "So there was a lot of coming and going," says Hartley, "which made us more self-sufficient." Or it could be a matter of money: as Hartley says, "I went to the film school I could afford." (128)

In addition to this production background, Hartley also studied with the noted early cinema scholar Tom Gunning, who has written the introduction to the published screenplay of *Flirt*. While I do not want to posit a direct correlation between Hartley's critical-studies education and his later career, we do see the influence of early cinema within his films in a more elaborate way when compared with the work of his contemporaries. Indeed, Hartley has made short films without dialogue and has expressed interest in making feature-length films without dialogue since *Trust* (1990). His actors often perform overly gestural movements that recall some early-cinema acting styles, especially in scenes of comic physical violence (Eaves; see also Gunning).

Purchase also is where Hartley initially connected with a group of regular collaborators with whom he has consistently worked. A portion of the "look" of Hartley's films can be attributed to the cinematographer Michael Spiller, who has shot thirteen of Hartley's productions dating back to their college days through 2001's *No Such Thing* (see Wood, *Pocket Essentials*, 110–11). The former Purchase students Nick Gomez and Hartley's cousin Bob Gosse have worked on and appeared in several of Hartley's early films, and the actors Robert John Burke, Dwight Ewell, Edie Falco, Parker Posey, Bill Sage, and Karen Sillas have played major roles in many of his films; Hartley tells *GreenCine* that Posey attended Purchase after him, but that his former professors alerted him to her (Eaves).

Not all of Hartley's collaborators are members of the Purchase Mafia, of course, including Brownstein; the producer Ted Hope, formerly of Good Machine and now of This Is That Productions; the production designer Steven Rosenzweig; and the editor Steve Hamilton of Mad Judy Productions, who, along with Hartley and Brownstein, started the postproduction house Spin Cycle Post in 1992. Hartley's perhaps most prominent non-Purchase collaborators are the actors with whom he has worked on multiple projects: Chris Cooke, Martin Donovan, Erica

Gimpel, Elina Löwensohn, John MacKay, Matt Malloy, D. J. Mendel, Chuck Montgomery, Miho Nikaido, Rebecca Merritt Nelson, Thomas Jay Ryan, Adrienne Shelley, Dave Simonds, James Urbaniak, and Damian Young. In 2006, Shelley, then working as an actor, director, and screenwriter, was murdered in a tragic incident in New York City. Two months after her murder, Shelley's film *Waitress* (2007) had its world premiere in the 2007 Sundance Spectrum, where Hartley's *Fay Grim* had its U.S. premiere (see Carr).

David Bordwell writes that "Hartley belongs to the more formally adventurous wing of the U.S. indie scene, a quality perhaps most evident in his storytelling strategies," his "idiosyncratic visual style," and his "disjointed and cross-purposes dialogues" (2–3). Hartley is associated with the American independent cinema of the 1980s to mid-1990s, a productive period akin to the New American Cinema or "Hollywood Renaissance" of the late 1960s to 1970s that saw the emergence of major directors as varied as Allison Anders, Kathryn Bigelow, the Coen brothers, Carl Franklin, Todd Haynes, Jim Jarmusch, Ang Lee, Spike Lee, Steven Soderbergh, and Gus Van Sant.[5]

Hartley writes and directs all of his films and works without big budgets and usually without major stars. It is perhaps to his credit as a director and as a judge of talent, however, that many actors who "started out" with him have gone on to more high-profile work. His directorial vision takes into account his own low-budget framework as aspects of his productions, not as hindrances, as long as he retains artistic control. As he tells John Fried, "I only have one rule: I'll take as much money from anybody who will give it to me as long as there are minimal strings attached" (Fried, "Rise of an Indie"). In an extension of the auteurist-indie ethos, Hartley writes and performs music for many of his films under the pseudonym Ned Rifle.

Hartley's films have been successful on the international film-festival circuit since the release of *The Unbelievable Truth,* which screened at the Sundance Film Festival when it emerged as the hub of American independent cinema, only a few years after the Sundance Institute took over the organization of the Utah/U.S. Film Festival. *Trust* won the 1991 Waldo Salt Screenwriting Award at Sundance, along with the Audience Awards at the Deauville Film Festival and at the São Paulo

International Film Festival. *Amateur* won the Young Cinema Competition Silver Prize at the 1994 Tokyo International Film Festival; *Henry Fool* won the Award for Best Screenplay at Cannes in 1998; and *Fay Grim* won the Audience Award for Best Narrative Feature at the 2007 RiverRun International Film Festival.

At least four major retrospectives of Hartley's work have taken place: at the International Film Festival Rotterdam in 1992; at the Gijón International Film Festival in Spain in 2003; at the ERA New Horizons Festival in Wroclaw, Poland, in 2007; and at Museo de Arte Contemporáneo de Castilla y León and the University of León in Spain from December 2009 to January 2010, which included the world premiere of *Possible Films 2*, Hartley's second DVD collection of shorts. Hartley was awarded the Chevalier de l'Ordre des Arts et des letters in 1997, and he taught filmmaking at Harvard University from 2001 to 2004. Hartley and his wife, Miho Nikaido, the Japanese actress and dancer who has appeared in several of his films, relocated to Berlin in 2004 when he was awarded a fellowship by the American Academy. I refer to Hartley's motion-picture output as "film," even though he has shot on film and on digital video.

Families and Bombs: The Long Island Films

The Unbelievable Truth

Hartley gradually amplified his experiments with cinematic style and narrative with *The Unbelievable Truth*, *Trust*, and *Simple Men*, the so-called Long Island Trilogy. Each film includes bombs as plot devices and enmeshes the protagonists within unusual romantic couplings and familial conflicts as they attempt to define themselves within and against their social contexts. Hartley's representation of these struggles leans toward the comedic, although dramatic and poignant moments do appear as he constructs the sometimes volatile intersection of private and personal matters with the public sphere.

The Unbelievable Truth depicts the burgeoning romantic relationship between Josh Hutton (Robert John Burke), a white ex-convict virgin in his late twenties, and Audry Hugo (Adrienne Shelly), a smart white teenager whose deep concern about nuclear annihilation manifests itself as the recurring sound of exploding bombs that only she hears. Hartley presents the relationship within a chronological yet imprecise timeframe that lacks temporal-spatial cues and uses all-caps intertitles—"AFTER A WHILE," "A MONTH MAYBE TWO MONTHS LATER"—to complicate matters. Josh and Audry are outsiders in their hometown of Lindenhurst, and they make unusual life choices: he is an expert mechanic who does not drive, while she has been accepted to Harvard University and is critical of consumer mass society but does not plan to attend college and instead becomes a fashion model who hawks luxury consumer goods. (Lindenhurst as the setting is unnamed by the characters, but it is announced on a movie-theater marquee.) As Caryn James summarizes, they are "two beautiful, somber-faced people dressed entirely in black . . . a perfect match [as] the weirdest . . . most sensible characters" in the film, but they do not know each other at its outset ("Applying 1950s Cool to the 80s," 11) (figure 1).

The combination of weird and sensible causes other characters to be threatened by Josh and Audry and to reduce them to essentialist types: Josh is a criminal, Audry is a crazy quasi-leftist, and their possible union might be catastrophic. This social scrutiny delays their romantic relationship for much of the film, primarily within Hartley's deployment of a

Figure 1: Audry (Adrienne Shelley) and Josh (Robert John Burke) in *The Unbelievable Truth*.

"bad-boy" narrative frame in which a mysterious, possibly violent man seduces a seemingly innocent woman into joining his risky adventures (e.g., *Badlands* [dir. Terrence Malick, 1973]). Within this narrative vein, the age difference between Josh and Audry generates concern about their romance, as does Josh's criminal past, which initially is known to all of the characters except Audry.

Once Josh and Audry meet, Audry's father, Vic Hugo (Christopher Cooke), hires Josh to work in his automotive garage as a favor to Audry and as a way to keep them apart. At the garage, Vic and fellow mechanic Mike (Mark Chandler Bailey) spy on Josh and identify him as a "mass murderer" who years ago dated Mike's girlfriend Pearl's (Julia McNeal) sister, killed her parents, and possibly killed Pearl's sister. In a later scene at the diner where Pearl works, Josh's story morphs as a waitress named Jane (Edie Falco) tells Mike, Audry's ex-boyfriend Emmet (Gary Sauer), and a fashion photographer named Todd (David Healy) that Josh "raped and murdered Pearl's older sister," "shot her father," and had a hand in her mother's disappearance. Todd corrects Jane with yet another version of the crimes, in which Pearl's sister "killed herself because her old man wouldn't let her marry [Josh, who] then went out after the old man and shot him. Then he went back and shot his *own* goddamn father!"

None of these stories tells the exact truth about Josh's past, which is that he killed Pearl's sister in a drunk-driving accident; a few years later, he pushed Pearl's father down a flight of stairs during an argument and killed him, the crime for which he went to prison. We eventually learn these details from Josh and Audry's mother, Liz (Katherine Mayfield), yet near the film's conclusion the story changes again when Pearl admits to Josh that she witnessed her father fall down the stairs on his own but blamed the death on Josh when she spoke with the police.

The "official" version of the truth that sent Josh to prison is not to be believed once Pearl's revelation is operative, even though Josh's criminal role in her sister's death is not in doubt. Pearl's revelation redeems Josh for the other characters at the film's conclusion and clears the way for Josh and Audry to have a "socially acceptable" relationship. Along with his newfound innocence, Josh's virginity allows Vic to create a neat fiction that sanctions the coupling as appropriate; Josh and Audry will not be sexually active, even though Vic knows that Audry has been sexually active with Emmet for years. This tenuously happy ending is one of the few to appear in Hartley's films, but it is balanced with an ominous tone. Josh picks up Audry and kisses her, but as they prepare to depart in Vic's van, she asks him if he hears a bomb, a question that is left unanswered as the camera tilts up to a bleak, blue-grey sky.

| | |

The Unbelievable Truth highlights Hartley's early antirealist vision through its jumbled timeframe, quirky narrative, and flat performance style for nearly all of the characters, a directing-acting strategy that we will see throughout his work. With the exception of Cooke's portrayal of Vic and some of Emmet's comic-violent outbursts, most of the actors drastically underplay emotional display when they face exciting, disturbing, dramatic, or tragic situations (on Cooke, see James, "Applying 1950s Cool to the 80s," 11). Audry worries about a nuclear holocaust but is not agitated when she hears bombs; although Pearl faints when she first sees Josh, his continued presence does not seem to bother her much. As Josh's past crime unfolds as a stuttered mystery, each version includes heightened unsettling elements that ought to alter character interactions, but none of the characters' tones, including Josh's, intensifies beyond matter-of-fact reporting (James writes that Josh's history is "not treated as melodrama, but as evidence of an unlucky fate" ["Applying 1950s Cool to the 80s," 11]). In such scenes, Hartley's characters are undisturbed and even dull. Their demeanors jar when compared to standards of realist drama, complicating our expectations about how characters are supposed to "act" within drama and tragedy.

Instead of the expected display of emotion and romantic exchange between Josh and Audry, Hartley uses the figure of George Washington as a decidedly unromantic foundation for their unconventional romance in what he calls "emotional commerce" (Fuller, "Finding the Essential," xvi). Hartley represents the first hints of Audry and Josh's romance about four minutes into the film with the unexpected juxtaposition of two images of Washington, shown first as John Quincy Adams Ward's bronze statue that stands in front of the Federal Hall National Memorial on Wall Street in New York City, the site of Washington's 1789 inauguration. The camera tilts away from an exterior medium-wide shot of the statue to a nearby intersection, as a gold 1950s-era sedan erratically enters the frame and comes to a stop. We have already seen the car pick up Josh as he hitchhiked from prison to Long Island during the opening credit sequence; he now exits the car and walks toward the statue. Josh is dressed in all black and carries what looks like an old-fashioned black medical bag—a look that aligns him with the dark bronze of the statue. After a few seconds, a quick shot/reverse-shot pattern cuts between Josh and Washington to suggest an impossible exchange of looks between them.

The second image of Washington follows when the film cuts from Josh and the statue to a direct-address close-up of a garish and rough color painting of Washington as he appears on the dollar bill. The camera maintains this shot for a few seconds before tilting down to Audry, who is stretched out on her bed with a concerned look on her face. A loud ticking and a rising, low hum play on the sound track, and when the camera rests on Audry, the ticking stops as an alarm clock rings. The hum continues just as she stretches her arms; with her arms above her head, she mouths an explosion that synchronizes with the sound of an actual explosion before she slowly lowers her arms in a gestural mimicry of the bomb (figure 2).

This "coincidence" of George Washingtons offers a slight contrast between Josh and Audry. The classical status of Ward's statue hints at Josh's desire for a return to a simple past or a status quo that does not exist for him, while the Warholesque quality of the painting hints at

Figure 2: Audry mimics a bomb in
The Unbelievable Truth.

Audry's more contemporary or unconventional approach to life. Beyond this contrast, though, Washington functions as a substitute for any declaration of love between Josh and Audry and as a representative of the honesty that comes to define them.

When Audry and Josh first meet, about fifteen minutes into the film, the two previous visual Washingtons give way to a discussion about the first president. Josh enters a thrift store to look for a book about Washington, and Audry, who hangs out at the store, tells him about her own interest in Washington, using a dollar bill as a visual aid: "I happen to be a big fan of George Washington myself. . . . He represents a lot of things I admire. For instance, he's singular. One. One dollar bill. Just look at him; he's not very attractive. But he's got dignity. He was a farmer. . . . Down to earth. And I can't help thinking that if he were alive today, doing the job he did then, leading that particular revolution, he'd be locked up. Or worse. All of them. Franklin. Paine. Jefferson. They'd be executed." When Josh doubts execution, Audry responds, "Don't put it past people. I don't trust anyone."

Audry's admiration of singularity and rebellion indicates much about her unconventional life within Lindenhurst's boundaries, and her general lack of trust plays with the prominent placement of Washington. Whereas the popular conception of Washington's "I cannot tell a lie" motto defines his personal virtue, Audry's "I don't trust anyone" announces an overarching skepticism that might, according to her logic, even cast doubt upon Washington's honesty. And yet Audry almost immediately trusts Josh, despite the rumors and facts that outline his past, most likely because he is guileless. Like many of Hartley's later characters, Josh and Audry defy the dishonest world of others and display their own unnerving and vulnerable honesty. They make little effort to guard their thoughts and often speak directly about their fears and desires. Josh revisits his past crimes and announces his virginity, while Audry advertises her aural bomb hallucination and asks others if they too hear the bombs, risking that they will view her as deranged. Indeed, some do. The bomb sound in Audry's bedroom at the film's outset muddles the diegetic and the nondiegetic and offers the possibility that the sound is real, something that the film never confirms.

Vic and Emmet believe that Audry has been warped by leftist propaganda and that her concern for the world is misdirected. Not surprisingly, both view her interest in Josh as an indication of her potential insanity. Jane repeatedly announces that she believes Audry is crazy, as in an entertaining scene late in the film that displays what Bordwell identifies as an example of Hartley's disjointed and cross-purposes dialogue:

JANE: I know what you need.
JOSH: Excuse me?
JANE: You need a woman.
JOSH: Oh.
JANE: That girl's crazy.
JOSH: I know, but I like her.
JANE: She's leaving town.
JOSH: I heard.
JANE: So come on. I know what you need. What do you say?
JOSH: Excuse me?

These lines repeat a few times before the film cuts away with the suggestion that this going-nowhere dialogue continues.

Along with the belief that Audry is crazy, the same characters believe that Josh is a dangerous man likely to kill again. But as with Audry's story, Hartley upends the fears about Josh with the simple premise that he is not aggressive, nor is he out to ruin Audry. Audry is far more active in seducing Josh, since she pursues him sexually, but he rebuffs her. Josh's chastity is notable when compared to realist cinematic depictions of male heteronormative sexuality as relentlessly focused upon sexual conquest of female partners. The fact that Josh is a virgin—a concept thought to be so unusual as to be the entire premise of Judd Apatow's *The Forty-Year-Old Virgin* (2005)—reframes his presence as a man "actually" interested in Audry as a person, not just as a sexual object. Josh also dodges Audry's advances out of respect for Vic, since Vic has warned him away from Audry—a warning that is part of Vic's inconsistent fatherly policing of his daughter's sexuality. Early in the film, Emmet tells Vic that he and Audry regularly have sex, and Vic attacks him. But later, Vic encourages Audry to become a model as a way to free him from financial commitments to her. This places Audry squarely within a sexualized/objectified profession and leads her to the predatory photographer Todd, who expects sexual favors in exchange for his help with her career. It is only when Vic sees nude photographs of Audry in a *New York Times Magazine* that he opposes modeling. In an interview with Graham Fuller, Hartley raises the possibility that Vic struggles to manage his own sexual interest in Audry (Fuller, "Finding the Essential," xxiii).

In contrast to Audry's sexual agency, Josh limits his sexual expression and leads a near-ascetic life once out of prison. He avoids Audry's romantic advances for much of the film, and a repeated joke supports a chaste air about him: people view his black clothing and his mechanic's bag as signs that he is a priest.[6] The stories about Josh's dangerous past, then, function as additional jokes about small communities whereby a person is misidentified by gossip and social scrutiny. Near the film's conclusion, in a scene at Josh's house, such surveillance reaches a climax of absurdity: Vic, Audry, Josh, and Mike enact a well-choreographed roundelay of suspicion and spying based upon the mistaken belief that Josh has slept with or harmed Pearl.

This is not to suggest that surveillance and gossip have no effect on Josh, since his chaste actions seemingly demonstrate the powerful influence of social scrutiny. Josh believes the gist of the stories about himself, thinks himself to be guilty, and acts accordingly, as Sophie Wise notes (257). Josh enacts sexual restraint with Audry because sexual activity might somehow add to his criminal guilt. For Audry, the bulk of scrutiny about her resides in the heteronormative, masculine monitoring of her sexuality and in the recurring questions about her sanity. Vic, Emmet, and Todd are preoccupied with Audry's sexuality and agency, and they more or less harass her in distinct ways. Yet while she is perturbed and unlike Josh, Audry manages to challenge the subject positions that are foisted upon her. She contests her father's arbitrary demands and rejects Emmet's and Todd's unwanted advances in order to pursue Josh and her own interests. As she maintains a certain amount of agency, initiates her life decisions, and deploys aspects of her subjectivity to her own advantage, Audry stands as a touchstone for the representation of female characters in Hartley's films, even when, as in *Trust*, this representational heritage does not seem present at first glance.

Trust

Trust depicts a condensed few days in the life of seventeen-year-old Maria Coughlin, also played by Adrienne Shelley, a character who shares Audry's age group but little else. Whereas Audry wears all-black and slightly baggy clothes, admires Washington, and is hyper–socially conscious, Maria is a model bad girl who favors heavily teased "big" hair, skintight neon fashion, and a "socially unconscious" disengagement with the world.

Trust's sharp and darkly humorous opening sequence intercuts a few static shots of Maria and her parents (Rebecca Merritt Nelson and Marko Hunt) with the film's stark titles, as we learn that she has been thrown out of high school for at least the second time. *Trust's* credits display the white-font-on-black-screen minimalist design that appears with some variation in all of Hartley's short and feature-length films—a "branded" frame.

Mr. and Mrs. Coughlin's anger is set against Maria's calm demeanor as she applies purplish-pink lipstick, lights a cigarette, and tells them that she plans to marry her boyfriend Anthony (Gary Sauer), who eventually will work for his father "pulling in a really bitchin' salary" (see cover image). As an afterthought, Maria announces that she is pregnant, which prompts her father to exclaim "tramp" and "slut" before he demands that she leave the house. Maria slaps him, half-yells "so there!" and exits just before her father collapses dead in the center of the frame. The Coughlins' other daughter, Peg (Edie Falco), arrives and confirms Mr. Coughlin's death, and the film cuts to its main title, with the addition of raucous rock music on the sound track.

From this sequence, the film moves to Matthew Slaughter (Martin Donovan), the other, less prominent protagonist, an angry, thirty-year-old white electronics genius. Matthew is obsessed with ethical propriety, which is on display when he first appears at his computer-manufacturing job. He destroys a computer, shouting that some things "shouldn't be fixed," before he quits because the company knowingly makes shoddy equipment. As a parting shot, Matthew locks his boss's (Matt Malloy) head in a table vice (figure 3).

From Matthew's outburst, the film returns to Maria and begins to crosscut between the characters' respective days until they first meet in a derelict house that evening. In Maria's scenes, we see Anthony reject her for getting pregnant, which prompts her to shop at a local boutique. While in a changing room, Maria notices her belly in the mirror, and it gives her pause. We next see her at an abortion clinic, where she schedules an appointment, and it is only when Maria returns home that she

Figure 3: Matthew (Martin Donovan) locks his boss's (Matt Malloy) head in a table vice in *Trust*.

learns that her father has died. Her mother banishes her for patricide, so she wanders the streets, narrowly escapes a sexual assault, and witnesses a baby kidnapping at a convenience store before she settles at the abandoned house.

Matthew's day is less dramatic, but it is still rough. After he quits his job, he returns home to his father's (John MacKay) demand to clean an already-spotless bathroom. Mr. Slaughter ostensibly hates Matthew, we later learn, because Matthew's mother died during childbirth, and the bathroom cleaning is one of his perverse punishments. After two attempts, the bathroom still does not meet Mr. Slaughter's standards, so he attacks Matthew in the first of several physical assaults on his son, and this abuse sends Matthew fleeing to the abandoned house.

Maria and Matthew's familial conflicts and dubious status as parent killers support Matthew's belief that "a family is like a gun. You point it in the wrong direction, you're gonna kill somebody." This sentiment functions as *Trust's* motto, but it is a sentiment that Maria and Matthew want to reverse as they attempt to reconfigure "family" as a nonviolent unit. Maria becomes introspective and begins to alter her life, Matthew searches for employment, and both admit that they have contemplated suicide. They quickly settle in to live together at the Coughlins' home, where Mrs. Coughlin outlines her plan for Maria's future. She will never forgive Maria for "killing" her husband, and she plans to "work [Maria's] fingers to the bone" as punishment—Mrs. Coughlin's penalty for perceived patricide also entails domestic duties. Notably, Hartley does not show anyone mourning Mr. Coughlin, and Mrs. Coughlin later admits that she "felt relief" when her husband died because he had "poisoned" her life. Maria is a "genius," she says, who removed her husband from the family with one slap.

After Maria's first appointment to have an abortion goes awry, Matthew concocts a plan to marry her and raise her child as his own (in a dissenting voice, Mrs. Coughlin tells Matthew that marriage "is a last resort"). Maria agrees to this, once Matthew signs on to her assertion "that respect, admiration, and trust equals love"—the unromantic notion that *Trust* advances against conventional wisdom about spontaneous, eternal love. It is within this spirit of suspicion about true love and with the background of Matthew's equation of families and guns that Maria and Matthew make tentative steps to create their new family. Yet unlike *The Unbelievable Truth*'s concluding coupling of Audry and Josh, *Trust* presents a rapid dénouement that acknowledges Maria and Matthew's difficult situation and subsequently centers upon the dissolution of their burgeoning romance.

Maria's new awareness of her subjectivity within the world encourages her to reconsider her plan to marry the near-stranger Matthew, so she has an abortion without his knowledge and halts their marriage plan. When Matthew finds out about the abortion, he rushes back onto his unstable path. He has another physical altercation with his father and returns to the computer factory to attempt a suicide bombing with a hand grenade, his father's Korean War souvenir that he always carries "just in case."

Maria, her family, and Mr. Slaughter follow Matthew, and when the grenade appears to be a dud, Maria rescues him by aiding his surrender. As they walk to the police, however, the grenade explodes but does not injure anyone. Instead, we see Maria and Matthew stretched out on the floor in opposite directions and facing each other in an abstract medium two-shot just before an off-screen police officer pulls Matthew out of the shot (an iconic image from Hartley's work; figure 4). The film jumps ahead to a shot of Matthew being taken away in a police car and then to

Figure 4: Maria and Matthew in *Trust's*
concluding moments, after the
grenade explosion.

its concluding shot of Maria, who stands alone in the middle of a deserted street, having survived the film's actual and figurative bombs.

| | |

Trust includes a similar level of stylistic experimentation as Hartley's first feature, coupled with a challenging narrative about Maria's transformation. Hartley jumps us into the film and Maria's life with no establishing shot to orient us, a technique that he repeats in the openings of most of his films. Maria's argument with her parents is at once generic and highly stylized—one of thousands of such conflicts between parents and a teenager, but presented with an abstract, shallow cinematography that complements Shelley's affect as she performs with little emotion. When we reach Mr. Coughlin's sudden death, Hartley's formal techniques convey just how off-kilter the rest of the narrative will be, as we see Maria gradually reverse the life plan that she outlines in the opening sequence (see Sarris 68; Kaufmann, "Billionaires"; Wise 245–46).

Maria becomes more introspective once she meets Matthew and becomes interested in expanding her intellect through reading and discussions with him. She radically changes her rather loud appearance into a plain, even ascetic style of straightened hair, no make-up, a drab blue housecoat that once belonged to Matthew's mother, Matthew's tan work boots, and eyeglasses that she had refused to wear in the past because they make her look like a librarian. Yet the start of Maria's self-examination begins when she makes her first trip to an abortion clinic, a raw scene before she meets Matthew and changes her appearance.

Unlike the abstracted kitchen in the film's opening sequence or the limited interior views of the computer factory, the clinic is shown in one of Hartley's rare exterior establishing shots. This shot also introduces Nurse Paine (Karen Sillas), who sits in a beaten-up green car and smokes a cigarette. As she leaves the car and crosses the street, the camera tracks to follow her as she enters the throng of protesters in front of the clinic. She next conducts an intake interview with Maria, in which Maria says that "there is no father" involved. Nurse Paine offers her a drink from a whiskey bottle that incongruously sits on her desk, before Maria speaks in a near-whispered monotone:

> You know, I'm looking at this guy, right? And I looked at him a lot before. So now I know that I have this little piece of him actually in me. Physically in me, and it makes me feel completely different, I don't know, sorta special or something. So I'm talking to him, I'm talking to him, and I realize, I'm, I'm talking to him, and I realize that he doesn't even see me. And I wonder what it was he was seeing when we did this. I go over it in my head, and I know now what he's seeing. It's really simple. He's seeing my legs. He's seeing my breasts. My ass. My mouth. He's seeing my cunt. How could I have been so stupid? That's really all there is to see, isn't it?

The structure and the troubling content of the monologue and Shelley's performance provide a profound counterbalance to the comedic moments that precede this scene, as Hartley offers us a challenging shift in tone. Unlike Audry's ability to withstand unwanted sexual advances and to negotiate the fraught world of a sexualized-objectified female teenager, Hartley first represents Maria's relationship to her sexualized subjectivity as distracted and unexamined—the general tone of her perspective about the world around her. Maria's awakening moment in the clinic is unexpected and marks the beginning of a more thoughtful, engaged phase of her life.

In *Upon Reflection: Trust* (2005), a documentary produced by Hartley's company Possible Films, Shelley and Hartley talk about how the abortion-clinic scene functions as Maria's rock-bottom moment and also a moment of "performance crisis" for Shelley:

SHELLEY: I didn't want to say the word "cunt." (Laughs)
HARTLEY: But you and Karen agreed, sort of like, "Yeah, a girl would never say that." And I had to really say, "Okay, I know that, actually, I know that a girl wouldn't say that, uh, but she has to." (Laughs)
SHELLEY: (Laughs). I was really scared of that, yeah, but it forced me to, you know, to be as still and as honest as possible. It forced me. I had to say a word I didn't want to say, and, you know, I had to say it as if I would say it.
HARTLEY: And it is a performance crisis or something. It comes across really moving, I think. I think she's really reduced to, you know, zero at that point; that was definitely a strategy of the storytelling. We're going to spend twenty minutes reducing this confident Long Island girl with big hair to nothing. And it's kind of cruel, in a way. And I always thought that that zero moment was that scene at the telephone booth when her friends even say, like, "No, you can't come over, my parents have heard what happened." But in fact, it seems like it happens in that moment.
SHELLEY: I think it does.

One additional reason that the abortion-clinic monologue is compelling, then, is that it hinges upon this realist-antirealist performance boundary. All involved in the production of the scene are uncomfortable, and although they are conflicted, Shelley and Hartley evaluate the scene as informed by the sense that it must happen for Maria's transformation to begin. Viewers in turn grasp this tension, the power of words in the scene, and its attendant painful and cruel elements.

A later scene that also presents a painful aspect of Maria's life takes place at the end of the film's second day of action, after she and Matthew have established themselves at the Coughlin house. Maria gives Matthew her bed, and as she prepares to sleep on the bare floor in keeping with her new ascetic life, she writes in a journal, "I am ashamed. I am ashamed of being young. I am ashamed of being stupid," which we see in a shot taken from her perspective. When juxtaposed with the abortion-clinic scene, this more private moment extends Maria's self-discovery and stands as an elemental portion of her "reconstruction" into a more engaged person. Maria commits to changing her life with this self-critical appraisal, and while she has become a virtual slave to her mother, she ironically starts to gain more agency, since she rejects her disengaged past.

Given Matthew's early decisive actions—he quits his job, couples with Maria, and devises a plan for their future together that "straightens out" his life—it seems that he too is prepared to change his life. He initially appears to be a conventionally sympathetic character whose abusive-father social context has marginalized him, and thus he is ripe for a new start. What makes this new start appear doubtful are the nagging hints about Matthew's commitment to any new direction for his life. He claims to want a new start with Maria and to abandon his father's tyranny, yet beyond quitting his job and settling in with Maria, few of his other actions indicate any real desire for change. It is not that he is deceptive per se, but rather that he is a static character who only *talks* of change with little ability to enact it. Hartley suggests as much during the precise, almost clinical depiction of Matthew's bathroom-cleaning saga: in the repetition of abstract close-up shots of him scrubbing the sparkling white tub, white sink, and white toilet, we detect that Matthew figuratively circles his own drain. He is stuck in lethargic repetition, and no amount of mindless work, attempts to please his father, ethical musings, or actionless plans to start a family will alter his circumstances.

Throughout *Trust,* Matthew's rut has a humorous yet sinister edge, a common narrative tone in Hartley's films. Whenever Matthew has an opportunity to change, he instead reverts to violence. His constant companion is a hand grenade, and his first and last actions in the film are grand, violent gestures that take place at the computer factory when he tries to destroy property and himself. In between these bookended scenes, Matthew has multiple altercations with his father, verbally threatens those around him (except Maria), and attacks a stranger (Bill Sage) at the abortion clinic when he accompanies Maria on her second of three trips. Matthew's delirious rage does not inspire confidence in Maria, and she realizes that his plan for marriage is shaky, yet unlike her reliance on Anthony at the film's outset, she is willing to set her own course without Matthew by the film's conclusion. Matthew in turn is left to the authorities in a reversed trajectory of Josh's narrative from *The*

Unbelievable Truth (Josh is one of the few male protagonists in Hartley's films to learn from his past and experience some form of change). Matthew is a more common type of man in Hartley's films, whose arrest, punishment, or exile belies his claims to a higher purpose or an ethically informed approach to life, as we see in *Simple Men*.

Simple Men

Simple Men is the final installment of Hartley's Long Island Trilogy, although unlike the previous two films, which were shot on Long Island, it was shot in Texas to lower costs. This film again represents familial conflict and uneasy heterosexual coupling as central stories, in this case following the exploits of Bill McCabe (Robert John Burke) and his younger brother, Dennis (Bill Sage). (Hartley's hour-length film *Surviving Desire* [1991] precedes *Simple Men* and also represents the uneasy romantic-couple theme, but without a familial context.)

Bill is a career criminal, and the film opens during a warehouse robbery in which his girlfriend, Vera (Mary McKenzie), a reddish-blonde woman whose appearance is reminiscent of Shelley's, double-crosses him to pursue love with their accomplice (James Hansen Prince). Heartbroken, Bill flees to New York City, where he by chance runs into Dennis, a meek student who is in the midst of a search for their estranged father, William (John MacKay), a former professional baseball star turned revolutionary fugitive. Their father has been living underground for twenty-three years because he is suspected of lobbing a bomb at the Pentagon, but he recently has been arrested in New York City. Bill joins Dennis's quest, and the two track their father to a hospital. He has had a stroke. When they arrive, they find the hospital swarming with police because their father faked his stroke to escape.

Bill does not share Dennis's interest in their father, but he joins his brother as a way to get out of the city. Their mother (Marietta Marich) gives Dennis a telephone number for his father that leads them to Long Island, where they have an eventful overnight stay in an abandoned Lindenhurst café across the street from a Catholic school; Lindenhurst is identified by a train-stop sign at their arrival. The brothers meet Kim (Holly Marie Combs), "a dangerously sexy thirteen-year-old," and Ned Rifle (Jeffrey Howard), the café owner who shares Hartley's composer pseudonym and is described in the published screenplay as *"a guy about thirty years old with the words 'missed opportunity' written all over his face"* (Hartley, *Collected Screenplays 1*, 285; on the history of the name Ned Rifle, see Wood, *Pocket Essentials*, 113).

Bill's time in Lindenhurst is spent getting drunk, outlining a deeply sexist plan to get revenge upon all women, and tutoring Ned in the ways of the world. During the film's opening moments, Bill takes a Virgin Mary medallion from the warehouse security guard (Richard Reyes), who repeatedly tells him, "Be good to her, and she'll be good to you." Bill does not recognize Mary but finds her to be "good looking" and in possession of a "nice personality," a sentiment that he passes on to Ned when he gives him the medallion. Just as George Washington guides *The Unbelievable Truth* as a signifier of emotional commerce, Mary circulates in *Simple Men* as a figure with an unspecified relationship to desire, which leads into one of Hartley's more well-known dialogue scenes when Ned trades his broken motorcycle for Bill's broken pistol and the medallion:

NED: I wish I could be more like you. . . . I want adventure. I want romance.
BILL: Ned, there's no such thing as adventure. There's no such thing as romance. There's only trouble and desire.
NED: Trouble and desire?
BILL: That's right. And the funny thing is, when you desire something you immediately get in trouble. And when you're in trouble you don't desire anything at all.
NED: I see.
BILL: It's impossible.
NED: It's ironic.
BILL: It's a fucking tragedy is what it is, Ned.

Bill and Dennis then flee the café on the repaired motorcycle just ahead of the police, while Ned accidentally fires off the pistol. A nun (Vivian Lanko) and a police officer (Matt Malloy) confront Ned after he fires the pistol, and he repeats, "There's nothing but trouble and desire" in a near-catatonic state. While Bill and Dennis escape on Ned's motorcycle, the nun and the police officer wrestle over Ned's medallion (figure 5).

After their escape, Dennis and Bill track their father's trail to Saga-

Figure 5: A nun (Vivian Lanko) and a police officer (Matt Malloy) wrestle for possession of a Virgin Mary medallion in *Simple Men*.

poneck and settle at a bar and restaurant that is owned by Kate (Karen Sillas), whose life's plan is to run her small business, to plant trees to repair the ozone layer, and to avoid her criminal and abusive ex-husband, Jack (Joe Stevens). (When Jack does return, he is a harmless, cowed man who is cold and in search of his jacket.) Kate's calm demeanor, simple life, and plain blue housedress also align her with the Virgin Mary and Hartley's other "saintly" women: Pearl in *The Unbelievable Truth,* the transformed Maria in *Trust,* Isabelle (Isabelle Huppert) in *Amateur,* and Beatrice (Sarah Polley) in *No Such Thing* (figure 6).

At Kate's, the brothers meet Elina (Elina Löwensohn), a mysterious, epileptic Romanian, and Martin (Martin Donovan), a local fisherman whose love for Kate is unrequited. With this configuration of characters in place, Dennis is drawn to Elina and correctly suspects that she is his father's girlfriend and is waiting for him at Kate's. Bill and Kate fall in love, and Bill vows to stay with her forever and abandons his revenge-upon-women plan. Martin turns out to be a secret follower of Dennis and Bill's father, and Mike and Vic (Mark Chandler Bailey and Christopher Cooke, respectively) from *The Unbelievable Truth* are relocated to the film as snooping local mechanics (see Fuller, "Finding the Essential," xxv–xxvi). When they call in the local sheriff (Damian Young) to investigate, he turns out to be a melancholic who longs for

Figure 6: Kate (Karen Sillas) in *Simple Men,*
dressed in a plain outfit that is reminiscent of the
costumes of other women in Hartley's films.

"an understanding without words. Dependence without resentment,"
before he asks rhetorically, "Why do women exist?"

It is almost as an aside that Dennis finally meets his father as the
film concludes. Mr. McCabe is about to flee the country with Elina and
Martin on Martin's boat, and Dennis finds them at a dock. Mr. McCabe
explains that he did not bomb the Pentagon, leads his followers in a
revolutionary call and response, and makes a plan to take Bill with him.
The sheriff arrives at Kate's around this same time, and she lies to cover
for Bill, which goes against her character, since it is rumored that she
has never told a lie, an echo of George Washington. Bill next arrives at
the dock and glares at his father before he rushes back to Kate's. Once
there, Bill rests his head upon Kate's shoulder in the film's final shot
and confirms his love for her. Offscreen, the sheriff says, "Don't move,"
providing the film with a peculiar circularity as he enunciates the same
phrase that Vera utters to a security guard at its opening.

| | |

Simple Men is a more developed antirealist film that advances on
Hartley's previous Long Island films' experimental strategies and compact
narratives and delivers on the promise of his much less straightforward

preceding short films, *Surviving Desire, Ambition,* and *The Theory of Achievement* (all from 1991). Caryn James notes that these short films take more chances with cinematic convention than his first two features, in which Hartley "crept a bit further away from realism [and point] toward the extreme stylization" of *Simple Men* (James, "Film View").

One clear link between the short films and *Simple Men* is Hartley's explicit use of choreography and dance, a process that he outlines in *Cineaste:* "I started with fight choreography in *Ambition,* one of my shorts. Once that was finished, I went straight into *Surviving Desire* and we developed the dance. Then, while we were making *Simple Men,* we said now let's do it with music" (Fried, "Rise of an Indie").[7]

Simple Men and *Surviving Desire* include notable dance sequences, the latter of which Hartley describes as an attempt to make "honest cinema" (Fuller, "Finding the Essential," xvii). This scene shows Jude (Martin Donovan) and two unnamed men dancing in a parking lot with no musical accompaniment just after Jude, a professor, is kissed by a female student (Mary B. Ward). As Hartley describes it, the dance eventually "introduces archetypal gestures that we were very conscious of: the grabbing of the crotch (where we were deliberately quoting Madonna, who was already quoting an existing cultural gesture herself), the crucifixion, *West Side Story,* etc. The dance is not disturbing particularly, but it is very emotionally confusing" (Fuller, "Finding the Essential," xvii–xviii) (figure 7).

While this dance seems out of place in the film, it does express Jude's emotional state, much like song and dance is used in standard realist musicals, enacting what Jane Feuer calls "the myth of spontaneity [where] musical performance [has a] spontaneous emergence out of a joyous and responsive attitude toward life" (443). The appearance of bands playing music at other moments in *Surviving Desire* also gives the film a musical feel, yet it is precisely because the film is not a musical that the dance-without-music is emotionally and generically confusing. The dance does not fit if we rely on genre convention, so we are left to comprehend it as something else, an overt interruption of the film that requires our more focused interpretation. Are the obvious allusions to musicals and notable performances only used to signify Jude's emotions in a splashy albeit clever manner? Must honest cinema forgo dialogue and continu-

Figure 7: The "crucifixion portion" of Jude's
(Martin Donovan) dance in *Surviving Desire*.

ity in favor of gesture and choreography as the vehicles of emotional
expression? Does this dance comment on the contrived nature of realist
musicals' spontaneous emotional displays?

These questions open up within *Surviving Desire* as interpretive possibilities for viewers, and it is this spirit that carries over to *Simple Men's*
even more elaborate dance. After Bill, Dennis, Kate, Elina, and Martin
form a group, the lead-in to the dance incongruously begins with a day-
time long take of Martin driving a small pickup truck down a dirt road
toward the camera. Birds chirp on the sound track, and as the truck skids
to a stop, the electric-guitar sounds that open Sonic Youth's "Kool Thing"
begin to build. Martin exits the truck, stomps to the center foreground,
and screams, "I can't stand the quiet!"—a sentiment that perhaps accu-
rately refers to his rural setting but contradicts the filmic moment, since
the song blares on the nondiegetic portion of the sound track.

From the quiet/not quiet scene of Martin's arrival, Hartley abruptly
cuts to a wide interior shot of a bar pavilion at night, where the song

becomes diegetic and functions as a sound bridge between shots. In Hartley's published screenplay, the dance scene in the bar reads:

INT. PAVILLION—NIGHT
Roaring rhythmic rock and roll fills the pavilion.
Tables have been upended.
Empty beer cans and bottles of booze line the bar.
Kate, Bill, Elina, Dennis, and Martin dance.
It's hot.
Steamy.
Sloppy.
Fun. (*Collected Screenplays 1*, 348)

These limited screen directions develop onscreen into a one-shot long take that uses exaggerated gestures instead of dialogue to construct the scene. Elina begins the dance with a sort of two-part performance: she stomps her feet, punches the air, and bends forward at the waist toward the camera in time with the music, and then alters her style into a lateral flowing movement in which she throws her head back (eyes closed, mouth open) and swings her arms out from her chest to her sides as though she is about to embrace someone.

Next, Dennis, who appears to be "sloppy" drunk, and Martin, who walks onscreen dragging a pool cue and holding a beer, watch Elina as she moves across the room left to right (the camera tracks on a diagonal to follow her). Elina ignores the men until she reaches the right side of the room and twirls around Dennis just as Sonic Youth's Kim Gordon begins to sing in a flat, terse tone, an affect that corresponds with the deadpan delivery of lines in Hartley's films. Dennis joins Elina as the song's chorus begins, and when the two dancers move back to Elina's original position and the camera retraces its movements, the second verse starts. Martin joins the dance from the top, and the three dancers make their way back right in a chorus line that resembles *Surviving Desire*'s dance (figure 8). Next, the song begins a spoken-word segment with Gordon and the rapper Chuck D, at which point the camera picks up Kate and Bill as they dance, embracing as a couple in the foreground. After a few beats, the camera moves back to the other three characters in their third iteration of the dance, during which Martin glimpses Bill and

Figure 8: Elina (Elina Löwensohn), Martin (Martin Donovan), and Dennis (Bill Sage) perform their chorus-line dance in *Simple Men*.

Kate, now offscreen. Before more action develops—is Martin planning to confront Bill?—the film jump-cuts into a low-angle medium close-up of Kate sitting at a table in the pavilion with no music playing on the sound track.

Hartley's use of dance is in line with conventional musicals, since the characters in *Simple Men* dance to express emotion—Bill and Kate's dance is shorthand for their mutual seduction, Martin displays his jealousy of Bill, and Dennis's interest in Elina is communicated though the dance. The bar space is demarcated with a division between the blue lighting of Bill and Kate (foreground) and more standard yellow light of the other three (background) to suggest that the two sets of dancers are in separate worlds. Bill and Kate sway close to each other and retain cool, erotically charged demeanors, while Dennis and Martin seem to be at sea as they try to keep up with Elina's wild movements. But like the dance in *Surviving Desire, Simple Men's* dance has a jarring effect because of its placement within a nonmusical film and because of its unconventional execution.

The dance is spontaneous, but Dennis and Martin do not display the skill that we usually see exhibited by dancers in traditional musicals as they "learn" the dance from Elina. Elina, while competent, does not have the carriage of a trained dancer, nor does her dance contain the hallmarks of professional choreography. Kate and Bill's rather mundane performance could be seen in films of any genre. In contrast to the dancers' performance, the cinematography of the long take is well choreographed, but it does not support an uninterrupted, unobstructed display of the dance-as-spectacle, since it moves off the first dance to film the second and then back again to the first. "Kool Thing" is an aggressive, well-known punk-noise song that complements Elina's dance style, but it runs counter to Bill and Kate's romantic embrace and seems out of place as the score for a dance number. Finally, Hartley undermines any sense of completion of the "production number" by cutting off the scene mid-song-and-dance with the contrasting conversation scene that follows.

Simple Men's dance is an homage to the café dance scene in Godard's *Bande à Part* (1964), in which two men (Sami Frey and Claude Brasseur) and a woman (Anna Karina) perform an unpolished, repetitive dance in one long take. In this scene, Godard unravels the myth of spontaneity with the use of an offscreen narrator (Godard himself) who interrupts the music to describe the feelings of the dancers and renders the signifying function of the dance explicit. Hartley references the content of *Bande à Part's* scene, its cinematography, and its tone with his own cinematography, which is more fluid than Godard's, with the setting of *Simple Men's* dance, with the threesome's clunky performance, and with the scene's attempts to rework musical conventions.

Added to this correspondence between films is the fact that Elina Löwensohn has more than a passing resemblance to Karina; the women wear similar blunt, dark bangs and have comparable facial features (figure 9). Löwensohn often is introduced into Hartley's films as an unnamed mystery woman, and I suspect that this aspect of her casting depends upon her great ability to perform enigmatic characters as comedic versions of Karina, Marlene Dietrich, or Greta Garbo. Additionally, Löwensohn's status within the worlds that Hartley constructs is "exotic," since her accented English and her distinct appearance mark her as "other" in comparison to the majority of women who populate his films.

The abrupt end of *Simple Men's* dance leads into another set-piece performance that, while not linked by action, is connected thematically to the dance and to the gender- and exploitation-focused lyrics of "Kool Thing." This scene also is set in the bar pavilion and is constructed of

Figure 9: Anna Karina in Godard's *Bande à Part.*

five close-ups of each character as they converse about music, gender, sexuality, and exploitation. The shots are cut together in a sequential order rather than a more standard shot/reverse-shot pattern, and the dialogue flows as an uninterrupted segment of time while the background sound is different in each shot, suggesting that the impression of dialogue continuity is misleading.

Kate opens this conversation when she says in a flat tone, "Madonna exploits her sexuality on her own terms." Offscreen, Elina asks, "What does it mean to exploit your sexuality on your own terms?" and Bill responds, "It means you name the price." Kate continues, "Madonna is a successful businessperson." Offscreen, Martin joins in with, "I like old-fashioned, straight-ahead rock and roll," before Dennis returns the conversation to Madonna, saying, "She sings okay." The conversation continues in a dull tone that stands apart from the energetic dances, and the five utter lines such as, "Everyone is involved with exploitation: the person whose body it is, the salesperson, and the audience that is entertained"; "Exploitation of sexuality has achieved a new respectability because some of the women whose bodies are exploited have gained control over that exploitation"; and, "But what about the audience?" Martin, who does not follow the gist of the conversation, is the last to speak. He reads from a sheet of paper as though he planned for this conversation: "Hendrix. Clapton. Allman Brothers. Zeppelin. Tull. BTO. Stones. Grand Funk Railroad. James Gang. T. Rex. MC5. Skynyrd. Lesley West. Blackmore. The Who—the old Who. Ten Years After. Santana. Thin Lizzy. Aerosmith. Hot fucking Tuna." He places the list in his coat chest pocket and looks around the table as though he has settled an argument before the film abruptly cuts to a shot of Bill and Kate slow dancing to a different song.

We understand that the conversation is a quirky digression within *Simple Men* that, like the dance, signals the developing relationships between the five characters. At the same time, the conversation, along with the dance and Martin's eruption before it, interrupts the film's more cohesive narrative and contrasts with its more naturalistic elements. Like the dance in *Surviving Desire,* these deliberate interruptions afford us opportunities to consider the cinematic construction of character motivation, narrative logic, and seamless temporality. How are we to make sense of the repeated temporal-spatial ruptures between the scenes—from day to night, from exterior to interior, and from invigorated dancing to staid conversation? What prompts Martin to erupt about silence, and how does his outburst connect with the musical explosion? Why does the conversation sound less like dialogue and more like a panel of experts in a documentary? (Martin is the dissenting voice on the panel and takes the conversation off topic when he argues for male-dominated rock as music for music's sake.)

As in *Surviving Desire,* these questions are not answered within *Simple Men* but instead open up interpretive possibilities for viewers. Such possibilities will vary depending upon a viewer's investment in cohesion or his or her familiarity with Hartley's oeuvre, but we may retrospectively understand this scene to be representative of a liminal moment between the first stage and second stage of Hartley's career. On one level, the conversation presents a brief extrafilmic consideration of the sometimes serious but usually humorous representations of objectification, sexuality, gender, and social roles in his first shorts and in *The Unbelievable Truth, Trust,* and *Simple Men.* On another level, the conversation anticipates threads of Hartley's more thoroughgoing and serious consideration of these and other topics in later films. Beginning with *Amateur*, Hartley moves into a new period that is marked by extended aesthetic interests and narrative expansion into the geography beyond Long Island and, eventually, beyond the earthly plane.

Obscenity and Espionage; or, "The Long Island Era Is Done"

Amateur

Amateur's narrative action moves from Long Island to New York City, marking the beginning of Hartley's sustained foray into locations beyond his home. In 1992, Hartley told Fuller, "The Long Island era is *done*. I started to make films in Long Island because that was the only place I *could* make films" (Fuller, "Finding the Essential," xxvi; some of his shorts are set in the city, as are scenes in *Surviving Desire* and *Simple Men*). Along with this locale shift, Hartley's narrative preoccupations move away from suburban family drama and social rebellion to a much darker escalation of violence and crime that is associated with the urban; ironically, after 1990, New York City has seen a decrease in the number of violent crimes (Hauser and Baker). Finally, in contrast to *Amateur*'s urban and modern setting, we also see Hartley's more explicit depiction of the metaphysical as it freely functions or seems to function in concert with his characters' everyday lives.

The film's urban crime emanates from Mr. Jacques, the head of "a highly respectable yet ultimately sinister corporation" with secret involvements in arms dealing, drug trafficking, and child pornography. Mr. Jacques is never shown in the film; as a structuring absence, he provides the motivation for other characters, most notably the protagonists, an amnesiac white man (Martin Donovan) and a red-haired virgin ex-nun named Isabelle (Isabelle Huppert). Huppert's casting alludes to her role as a prostitute named Isabelle in Godard's *Sauve Qui Peut (la Vie)* (Every Man for Himself; 1980) and continues Hartley's visual-typecasting, since she resembles Shelley, Sillas, and Mary McKenzie (figure 10).

Isabelle believes that she is an uninitiated nymphomaniac and has left the convent to write pornography, even though her publisher, George

Figure 10: The ex-nun and self-proclaimed virgin
nymphomaniac Isabelle (Isabelle Huppert)
in *Amateur,* with a billboard icon of the
Virgin Mary in the background.

(David Greenspan), fears that her work is too poetic. Once Isabelle meets the amnesiac stranger, who is revealed to be a pornographer and a former employee of Mr. Jacques named Thomas Ludins, she asks him to make love to her so as to fulfill her destiny as a nymphomaniac. He agrees, but for various reasons, their plan gets delayed throughout the film; for a film centered on sexuality, *Amateur* includes no "explicit" sexual images. Thomas has forgotten his own reasons for being in New York City, which are to stalk his estranged wife, Sofia (Elina Löwensohn), a world-famous porn star who has fled from Mr. Jacques and him, and to blackmail Mr. Jacques with computer disks that outline the corporation's illegal activities. Sofia meanwhile believes that she has killed Thomas just before the film opens, and she seeks help from Edward (Damian Young), an accountant partner of Thomas's who also is on the run from Mr. Jacques.

Thomas's search for his identity intersects with Sofia's new life and with what Isabelle conceives of as her unspecified, painful divine mission, which has been given to her in lifelong visions of the Virgin Mary.

The visions are not included in the film, but the Virgin Mary does appear as an icon that hangs in Isabelle's sparse apartment and as a partial mother-and-child Renaissance painting on a billboard advertisement (see figure 10). Thomas does not believe in Isabelle's mission but rather believes that they have been brought together through "really bad luck." He and Isabelle gradually surmise that he has some relationship with Sofia because Isabelle coincidentally sees her at a porn theater and because Thomas sees pornographic still and video images of Sofia that spark some faint recognition. Isabelle thus fixes upon the idea that her mission is to help Sofia break away from Thomas.

While this character configuration provides plenty of wacky comedy, Hartley rapidly mixes in scenes of violent drama. Thomas's amnesia characterizes him as a placid figure within the film's present time, but Sofia and Edward remember him as a vicious man who "cuts up" and drugs women who are unwilling to appear in his pornographic films. Once Sofia realizes that she possesses Thomas's floppy disks—which she and other characters note are neither floppy nor disks—she adopts Thomas's blackmail plan and unfortunately draws the attention of Mr. Jacques's two New York–based accountants-cum-assassins, Jan (Chuck Montgomery) and Kurt (Dave Simonds). Jan and Kurt hunt Sofia but instead capture Edward, torture him, and leave him for dead. Yet like Thomas, Edward has a resurrection and transforms into a violent, deranged mute bent on protecting Sofia—he attacks strangers and kills a New York City police officer in scenes that simultaneously are slapstick and disturbing.

Eventually and independently, Sofia and the deranged Edward learn that Thomas is alive and reluctantly join with him and Isabelle against Jan and Kurt. The assassins track different configurations of the foursome until Jan shoots Sofia in the shoulder and is in turn killed by Edward in a highly staged moment of absurdist, comedic brutality near the film's conclusion.[8] Isabelle sends the disks to her publisher, a wannabe investigative journalist, in an apparent conclusion of the Mr. Jacques plotline. The group retreats to Isabelle's former convent to get Sofia medical treatment. There, Sofia reveals Thomas's identity to Isabelle while she awaits transportation to a hospital for further treatment. Isabelle then meets Thomas in a covered stone passage of the convent but does not yet relay the information about his identity. He leaves her to retrieve a car for

Sofia's transport, and Isabelle gives him a loaded handgun in a gesture of trust—earlier she had given him the same gun after secretly unloading it because of her lingering doubts about him. With gun in hand, Thomas opens the large convent door, where he mistakenly is shot dead by the police who pursue Edward, a sudden final action that ends the film.

| | |

Amateur's depiction of Thomas grounds a philosophical notion of split subjectivity within the actual division between his buried past and his amnesiac present. Here, Hartley's cinematic play with abstract or theoretical concepts suggests that a unified, essential identity is impossible, as does his depiction of Isabelle's multifaceted subjectivity as virgin-nun-visionary-nymphomaniac-pornographer. Similarly, Hartley represents Thomas's amnesiac life as a rebirth or resurrection so that he functions in the film's present as a new man without conscious connections to criminality and pornography.

We know little about Thomas's past, and the most complete version that the film includes comes from Sofia, who wants to be "a mover and a shaker," now that Thomas is dead. Sofia summarizes her past with Thomas for Edward at the film's midpoint: "I hate [Thomas]. He took advantage of me. He got me hooked on drugs when I was twelve. He put me in pornographic films. I'm sick of it. I want to change my life. He won't let me. I'm unhappy. I pushed him out a window. I killed him." Sofia narrates the events that immediately precede the film's first enigmatic image of Thomas stretched out on his back in a cobblestone alley. (Jason Wood points out this image of Donovan on a cobblestone street is virtually the same image that concludes *Surviving Desire* [*Pocket Essentials*, 6].) Sofia furtively approaches the body, taps it with her foot, and exits the alley—actions that suggest that Thomas is dead and that she does not want to be involved and/or is not concerned enough to report it.

It is a surprise when, a moment later, Thomas's eyes flash open, and he rights himself into a low crouch (figure 11). On the sound track, we hear Isabelle's unidentified voiceover say, "And this man will die. He will. Eventually," before Hartley cuts from the now-alive Thomas to Isabelle, who sits at a diner counter and types onto a laptop computer. She reads aloud what she writes: "'He will die,' she repeated, 'and there is nothing any of us can do about it.'" Her in-progress text then shifts from the dead man to a sexual encounter between a woman and a man, which creates a stir among the other patrons in the diner just as Thomas walks in, bleeding at the back of his head and in possession of no identification. Isabelle buys Thomas a sandwich and then takes him back to her apartment, beginning their relationship. With Isabelle identified as the source of the brief voiceover, before she meets Thomas, we might surmise that the images set in the alley are imaginative illustrations of the text that she writes with Thomas as her character. Thomas's arrival at the diner as the resurrected amnesiac amends this idea, however, and the fiction-within-a-fiction is set aside.

Isabelle is not wary of Thomas and sets out to care for him at once, but she does have a small reservation about him that develops throughout the film—she is in touch with the metaphysical, after all. Isabelle's nagging impression is that Thomas has a violent past, a feeling that is supported when she overhears him shouting in his sleep about Sofia and about attacking women. Once Sofia appears in Isabelle's life, this impression grows. Sofia obviously fears her ex-husband when she sees that he is alive, and she initially refuses to reveal her connection to him

Figure 11: Thomas (Martin Donovan) awakens on a cobblestone street in *Amateur*'s opening.

or to name him. It is only at the convent that Sofia provides Isabelle with Thomas's identity and elements of his past on the condition that she never wants to see him again.

This crucial conversation between Sofia and Isabelle, like Sofia's initial fight with Thomas that provides the catalyst for the film, is not shown, so we are left with only a generalized sense of Thomas's violent past. Hartley instead presents Isabelle's reaction to Sofia's information when she meets Thomas in the hallway. Her face indicates that what she has learned is troubling, and Thomas notices and apologizes, even though he does not know what he apologizes for, as Isabelle points out to him. Isabelle patches over the tension and reassures him by asking if he will still make love to her. A stylistic flourish of cutaways of Edward and Sofia delays Thomas's response, which is to kiss Isabelle and say "eventually"—an echo of her earlier words about his death—before he leaves to get a car for Sofia.

Hartley does not present a clear-cut sense of space after this meeting, but in the shots that follow, Isabelle discovers that the New York City police have arrived at the scene and chases Thomas through the convent to warn him. When she stops and yells "Thomas!"—the only time in the film that he is addressed by name—the film juxtaposes her concerned expression with his ease as he unlatches the large double-doors at the convent entrance and slowly turns toward her. Although Thomas does not know his name, he seems to understand that Isabelle is hailing him; when he turns fully around toward her, the doors swing open to reveal a crowd of police officers crouched behind their cars with their guns drawn. One officer shoots Thomas. The film cuts to Isabelle's reaction shot and then to a police officer who approaches Thomas, rolls his body onto his back, and says, "This isn't him," indicating that they had intended to shoot Edward. After Thomas is shown stretched on the cobblestones, Isabelle kneels next to him as an offscreen officer asks, "Do you know this man?" Isabelle answers, "Yes, I know this man," before the film cuts to black in a heavy punctuation moment before the closing credits roll.

When Isabelle answers the officer's question, she picks up the phrasing of her first words spoken in the film—"this man"—to fold back onto the film's opening, which foreshadows Thomas's character's arc. This linguistic return suggests just how much Isabelle's mission to aid Sofia coincides with her crucial role in Thomas's preordained death. Here, the

Figure 12: *Amateur*'s conclusion: Thomas dead on the cobblestone in front of Isabelle's former convent, with the police noting that they have shot the wrong man.

film's narrative logic fulfills Isabelle's sense that her mission will cause her pain, which in turn strengthens her belief that her visions are divine and that her involvement with Thomas is not "really bad luck."

Further advancing this impression of destiny fulfilled are the film's final images of Thomas. We see the assuredly dead man stretched out on yet another cobblestone surface in a visual echo of *Amateur*'s opening moments (figure 12). Along with the fulfillment of Isabelle's opening lines, these visual bookends retrospectively frame Thomas as a "dead man walking" throughout the film. This reading recalls Billy Wilder's *Double Indemnity* (1944) and anticipates aspects of Jim Jarmusch's *Dead Man* (1995). Though not an amnesiac, *Dead Man*'s William Blake (Johnny Depp) is a bit of a blank slate. Like Thomas, he meanders through his final days with the aid of a new companion, Nobody (Gary Farmer), a metaphysical figure who occupies a position similar to Isabelle's in relation to Thomas, if we consider that Nobody and Isabelle "guide" Blake and Thomas toward their deaths. *Amateur* does not include flashbacks like Wilder's film as a way to contextualize the dead man's crimes within a temporal setting, yet Hartley still imbues Thomas with a haunted past that has much to do with his own criminal actions. Just as Walter Neff (Fred MacMurray) cannot escape his past in *Double Indemnity*, Thomas is unable to shake his own bad deeds. Even though Thomas's death is the result of mistaken identity—he is not the target of the police—it functions as misaligned retribution for his previous actions and simultaneously functions as one of the more moving sequences to appear within Hartley's work.

Henry Fool

Location, similar themes, and some minor characters act as the glue for Hartley's Long Island Trilogy. With *Henry Fool* and *Fay Grim*, we see a formally linked first film and its sequel, perhaps the first two installments of a mythic serial narrative that Hartley and others jokingly have compared to the *Star Wars* series (see Fuller, "Responding to Nature," xviii; *Higher Definition with Robert Wilonsky*).

Henry Fool opens with a garbageman, Simon Grim (James Urbaniak), his unemployed sister, Fay (Parker Posey), and their depressed, shut-in mother (Maria Porter) as they slog through life in Woodside, Queens. When the mysterious stranger Henry Fool (Thomas Jay Ryan) arrives and rents a basement apartment from them, everything changes for the Grims. Simon does not speak much and has no friends at the film's outset, so Henry gives him a blank composition notebook so that he might write when he "can't get it out." Simon fills the notebook overnight with an epic poem that he inadvertently has written in iambic pentameter, and thereafter he quits his job to devote all his time to poetry, which Henry promises to promote to an "old friend," the publisher Angus James (Chuck Montgomery).

Henry delays this promise, which eventually prompts the neophyte writer to demand a meeting with Angus without Henry's assistance. After Angus reads Simon's work, he offers an amusing, demoralizing rejection:

> This is really quite unbelievably bad, my friend. I mean, I'm all for experimentation and I've made a career out of a healthy disregard for convention, but look, this is profoundly irrelevant material. This is only my opinion, but it's an opinion I value highly. I've been wrong before as

a publisher, but I refuse to admit that I've ever been wrong as a reader. You have talent, I admit. You have an innate sense of the musicality of language, a good ear maybe, but you do nothing significant with it. And this twisted reasoning that poses as conviction or insight, it's, well, it's embarrassing.

Angus's critique devastates Simon, but the coup de grâce comes when the publisher tells him that he's never heard of Henry Fool. Angus's assistant (Veanne Cox) then tells Simon that Henry is no friend of Angus's but that he had been a janitor at the publishing house.

Henry's promise to Simon is unfulfilled because Henry is a "brilliant bullshit artist" who is too busy loitering and sexually pursuing the Grim women (Thomas Jay Ryan in *Higher Definition with Robert Wilonsky*). He first plans to seduce Fay but gets distracted and instead has sex with Mrs. Grim, which Fay witnesses; Mrs. Grim later accuses Henry of rape, a claim her family ignores. Later, Fay sneaks into Henry's apartment and reads portions of his memoir. Henry discovers her, and they have exaggerated, comic, and slightly violent sex just as Simon returns from his meeting with Angus to discover Mrs. Grim's body upstairs. She has committed suicide after reading Simon's poem, which might have encouraged her to reflect upon her failed career as a pianist.[9]

Added into the family drama is Fay's pregnancy, the result of her basement dalliance with Henry. After Henry drinks too many espressos and learns from Simon that Fay is pregnant, he whines that he has let himself be caught in the "bloody maw of banal necessity" and rushes to the bathroom where Fay showers. In a gross scene of actual bathroom humor, Henry has a disgusting, excessive bowel revolt while he simultaneously holds what he believes to be a gold ring that he found in the garbage. Simon correctly identifies the ring as a gasket from a refrigerator hose, but Fay, like Henry, sees it as jewelry and misinterprets Henry's frantic actions as a nervous marriage proposal, even though he is sitting on the toilet.

Henry's only admirable act in relation to Fay is to distract her from the suicide by asking her to upload Simon's poem onto the World Wide Web (unlike *Trust*, *Henry Fool* presents a bit of mourning for the dead parent). In conjunction with the conclusion of their wedding ceremony, they learn that Henry has inadvertently kept his promise to Simon since

Simon's poem has become an Internet sensation, which attracts Angus's attention. No man of conviction, Angus agrees to publish the poem because "other people's responses [are] proof of [the] poem's appeal," while Simon makes an ill-conceived deal with Henry: if Henry will let Simon read his *Confession*, Simon will insist that Angus publish it along with his own poem. Simon unfortunately makes this deal before he reads the terrible memoir. Once Angus reads it, he calls Henry a "scoundrel" and refuses to publish it. Faced with this opposition, Simon breaks his own promise to Henry in favor of his career in the decisive break in their relationship, which takes place at a hospital after Fay and Henry's son Ned is born.

The film then jumps ahead seven years to its conclusion. Henry has taken over Simon's job as a garbageman and has made a halfhearted attempt to commit to Fay (on this seven-year jump in relation to novelistic representation, see Justin Wyatt's interview with Hartley in this volume). No careful father, Henry introduces seven-year-old Ned (Liam Aiken) to the world of strippers, drinking, and smoking, while an estranged and reclusive Simon is about to be awarded the Nobel Prize for Literature.

A plotline quickly develops in which Henry's fourteen-year-old neighbor, Pearl (Christy Carlson Romano), asks him to kill her sexually abusive stepfather, Warren (Kevin Corrigan), in exchange for oral sex. Although Henry seems disturbed by Pearl's proposition, he does scuffle with Warren and stabs and kills him (perhaps in self-defense). Henry goes into hiding, and Ned, an intrepid seven-year-old, tracks down Simon at a hotel (the published screenplay identifies it as the famous outlaw-artist domain, the Chelsea Hotel). There is little onscreen deliberation about Henry's escape plan as Simon nearly wordlessly repays Henry's early support and escorts him to an airport. Henry poses as Simon in order to flee to Sweden, but before any successful escape is shown, the film ends with an ambiguous framing of Henry's inconclusive actions.

| | |

Part Devil, part Falstaff to Simon's Prince Hal, Henry is, like Thomas from *Amateur*, a bad man with a violent, mysterious past (Fuller, "Responding to Nature," xi, xiv–xv). Henry readily admits that he has been to prison for a statutory-rape conviction but admits little else, and while he does not produce pornography like Thomas, he has an interest in pornography because he "learns so much" from it. While the reasons for their shrouded pasts differ—Thomas's is the result of amnesia, Henry's is the result of deliberate fabrication and evasion—Thomas and Henry are characters whose appearances radically change the lives of those around them.

Henry arrives in an early scene where Simon appears unwell and leans against a chain-link fence in front of the Grim house, while Fay, dressed for a night out on the town, utters, "God, I want to get fucked," before she departs. As the camera moves around Simon, a minimal, nondiegetic percussive keyboard and the sound of thunder on the sound track jars with the placid images of an otherwise sunny day. Simon re-acts to these sounds by placing his ear to the pavement, a reaction that complicates the nondiegetic status of the music and the aural presence of thunder in the scene, before Hartley cuts to the opening credits. Henry then marches into a wide shot of a sunny, tree-lined street from the background, dressed in a rumpled three-piece suit and carrying two brown leather suitcases.

Hartley visually conveys much about Henry's darker aspects in this scene. The cinematography positions the street as a low horizon line in Henry's first shot, so that he appears to ascend as a demon arriving from the underworld (figure 13). As the scene continues, Henry rents the Grims' basement apartment, and its mise-en-scène advances his de-monic air. The subterranean den has grey cement walls covered in large splotches of red paint, is lit by the red glow of the woodstove, and recalls cinematic representations of torture chambers or serial-killer hideouts.

Once settled at the Grims,' Henry's actions only add to the fiend-ish impression that surrounds him. Ryan's performance fits within the restrained acting style dominant within Hartley's films, but with slight alterations. Ryan-as-Henry emotes more passion in a conventional way when compared with Hartley's other actors, yet he still maintains a cer-tain blankness in his staccato delivery of lines, in his facial expressions, and in his interactions with other characters. As such, Ryan embodies Henry's maniacal energy as a man possessed who first sets out to instruct Simon in the art of writing as an outlaw enterprise.

This instruction begins about eight minutes into the film, in Henry's new apartment, where Henry lectures Simon in a tone that is at once

Figure 13: Henry's (Thomas Jay Ryan) arrival, seemingly from the underworld, with his *Confession* in his suitcases in the opening moments of *Henry Fool*.

matter-of-fact, professorial, and agitated (transcribed here with Simon's short lines omitted):

> I go where I will, and I do what I must. That's why I'm in trouble. I'm sort of what you might call in exile. . . . An honest man is always in trouble, Simon. . . . [These notebooks are] my life's work. My memoirs. My *Confession*. . . . I've been bad. Repeatedly. But why brag? The details of my exploits are only a pretext for a far more expansive consideration of general truths. What is this? It's a philosophy. A poetics. A politics, if you will. A literature of protest. A novel of ideas. A pornographic magazine of truly comic-book proportions. It is, in the end, whatever the hell I want it to be. And when I'm through with it, it's going to blow a hole this wide straight through the world's own idea of itself.

Unlike Josh in *The Unbelievable Truth*, Henry does not take on a societal view of himself that positions him as a guilty man. Rather, his shady past and bad activities are revolutionary. Henry subsequently outlines the contours of his work and its likely impact to construct his identity and posit that there can be no distinction between one's work/art/vocation and one's subjectivity. But what motivates Henry to invest in Simon? "An honest man is always in trouble" is Henry's motto, but we see that his honesty is open to question for much of the film; the truth of his philosophy and his actions hews to self-involvement in the extreme. Henry's altruism toward Simon readily contrasts with his self-involvement and is complicated further because, when he and Simon meet, Simon expresses no interest in writing. It is Henry's initiative to "save" Simon through writing, even though it is difficult to imagine that Henry wants to save anyone.

A more likely interpretation of Henry's involvement with Simon is that he desires to cultivate an acolyte, not to mention an acolyte who has a room to rent. Simon is the perfect student in this scenario, since he apparently knows nothing about literature or, as Henry notes, grammar, and he initially will not scrutinize the details of Henry's past exploits. Hartley depicts Simon's belief in Henry's abilities and history as genuine, and he sees his mentor as an inspiring artistic outlaw. With the representation of Simon's success, Hartley complicates Simon's belief in Henry to comment on difficulties that might arise within the production of artistic material, mentorship, and inspiration. Simon takes Henry's guidance more seriously than Henry himself and outperforms his mentor, which in turn undermines Henry's initial reasons for cultivating Simon as an acolyte. Simon takes risks and devotes himself to writing and publication in ways that Henry does not. Unlike his mentor, he also produces work that has the possibility of being read by the public.

This is not to suggest that Henry plays no role in Simon's success but rather that he does so in a haphazard way. Henry, of course, inspires Simon to write and offers critiques of Simon's work, and he is the first to circulate Simon's poetry when he inexplicably tapes a page of it near the cash register at the local hangout, World of Donuts. From this action, Hartley advances outrageous incidents to track the divergent impact of Simon's work, starting with Gnoc Deng (Miho Nikaido), the young mute Asian woman who works at the donut shop that is owned by her father (James Saito). Gnoc reads Simon's poem and begins to sing and cry, which her father understands to be a happy, almost miraculous response.

An opposite response comes from a waitress named Vicky (Jan Leslie Harding), Pearl's mother and Warren's future wife, who supports a right-wing, culture-warrior congressional candidate named Owen Feer (Don Creech). Vicky reads one page of the poem taped near the register and immediately labels it pornography, but notably does not comment upon the pornographic magazines displayed across an entire wall at the front of the shop. Vicky's response reverses the logic applied to Isabelle's pornographic writing in *Amateur;* Isabelle writes pornography that reads as poetry, while Simon writes poetry that is taken to be pornographic. After Vicky and Gnoc stake out two responses to Simon's work, his notoriety mushrooms. Local students decide to publish a portion of the poem in their school newspaper, which provokes reactions from parents and the school board, who label it "scatological" and, again, pornographic. A newspaper reporter (Marissa Chibas) next tells Simon that "the county agrees with the church and considers the poem emblematic of modern society's moral disintegration," and established editors roundly reject it, one going so far as to write to Simon, "Drop dead. Keep your day job." When Henry again circulates Simon's work online, the poem inspires students to burn down a school and receives a critique from the Pope, who, according to a television news report, "offer[s] a prayer for the young, whom he describe[s] as sadly in need of faith and not the illusion of conviction offered by rock music, drugs, and contemporary poetry."

Given this global spread of Simon's poetry, it is comical as well as frustrating that Hartley never allows us to read or to hear the poem. The same situation applies to Henry's *Confession,* so we must rely upon other characters' mediated readings of these texts to frame our sense of the writers' literary output and persona, thematic interests, and style. Henry is a scoundrel, an outsider philosopher, or a bad writer, while Simon is a pornographer, a visionary, or an accidental poet. These interpretations, of course, tell us nothing about Simon's poetry or Henry's memoir, and Hartley's refusal to provide direct access to their work highlights other difficulties related to artistic production and distribution. Censorship, institutional acceptance and approval, and audience interests might obstruct *or* allow for distribution in a strange amalgam characterized as "market conditions." The actual quality or content of the material might not matter, and its producer's efforts might have little influence over distribution.

We see the obstruction and eventual distribution of Simon's poem in *Henry Fool* as Hartley reveals a prescient sense of the Internet as a new, potentially more open channel of distribution.[10] Simon's poem gets "legitimate" or institutional publication only after Angus, a gatekeeper of literary culture, embraces his work via the stir or "buzz" that it creates on the Web. Angus presumably still finds the poetry to be profoundly irrelevant and embarrassing, but now it is marketable. Since Henry does not benefit from any buzz, Angus is willing to reject it, just as he once had done with Simon's poem.

What had worked for Simon does not work for Henry, since Henry has no advocate, a role that Simon fails at when given the opportunity. Simon's only support for Henry comes when he escorts his former mentor to the airport. Henry appears confused and even hesitant in this portion of his escape, and his temperament suggests that he has second thoughts about leaving his family. Simon urges him to leave the terminal, but Henry's reluctance persists. When Henry does leave, Hartley cuts up his actions with shots of the plane to confuse screen direction and spatial arrangements. He stops on the tarmac and looks between the plane and the terminal, and then is shown, in the film's final abstract shot, running on the tarmac and carrying the two suitcases that contain his *Confession*. While buildings and a plane appear in the background, no clear screen direction is indicated by the construction of the shot or the editing (figure 14). Before any resolution to Henry's actions is

Figure 14: The final shot of *Henry Fool,*
in which Henry's indeterminate actions
mask the possibility of his escape.

shown, the film cuts away to a punctuating shot of black that leads into to the final rolling credits.

Given Henry's hesitation in the terminal and the abstraction of his final actions, we might wonder whether he is headed toward the airplane, or if he has had a change of heart and has decided to return to his family and face criminal prosecution. These conflicting interpretations are a well-known part of the film's extrafilmic discourse and are built into the doubts about Henry's escape that are expressed by characters at *Fay Grim*'s outset (see *Higher Definition with Robert Wilonsky*). With the conclusions of *Trust, Simple Men,* and *Amateur* in mind, it is reasonable to imagine that Henry will not or cannot escape judicial authority. We might interpret his actions to be like Bill's in *Simple Men,* who follows his romantic inclinations, or as a reckless action like Matthew's in *Trust,* both of which result in arrest. Or, like Thomas in *Amateur,* we might believe that Henry cannot avoid punishment for his past misdeeds— he has been bad, repeatedly—even if punishment in this instance is weighed against his attempt to protect Pearl. The screen directions in the published screenplay, however, tell a different story: *"Henry is running, struggling towards us, forcing himself towards the plane, getting stronger and running faster with every step he takes"* (Hartley, *Henry Fool,* 153). Henry is determined to escape from the authorities *and* from his family, who embody the "bloody maw of banal necessity," and it is this determination that shapes *Fay Grim*'s trajectory.

Fay Grim

Fay Grim opens seven years after *Henry Fool*'s conclusion and adds a post–September 11 spy-film parody to the family comedy-drama of the series. Simon is in prison for his role in Henry's escape, and Fay is raising an increasingly troublesome Ned, who might be following in his father's louche footsteps. (Together, the two films encompass approximately fourteen years in the main characters' lives; I will note actors new to the second film only.) Henry's whereabouts are unknown, and Simon's role in Henry's escape has generated a new public interest in *Confession,* but Simon suspects that this interest is more sinister.

Fay is drawn into new intrigue related to Henry in the film's first three scenes. At a church, Father Lang (D. J. Mendel) counsels her about Ned as she notes that she knows very little about her estranged husband. Since she easily recalls Henry, perhaps Fay's concern about Ned is another way to articulate the major question that hangs over the film: just who is Henry Fool? Fay next receives a cellphone call and moves on to meet Ned's rigid principal (Megan Gay). Ned has been caught at school with an ornate, red-and-gold, antique-looking hand-held precinematic toy that shows a motion-picture loop of an orgy; it had arrived in the mail addressed to him. The principal shows it to Fay and links it to the Fool-Grim family's historical transgressions, which Fay briefly discusses as she views the orgy (figure 15). Fay's phone rings again and moves her along to a meeting with Angus and his assistant, Milla (Jasmin Tabatabai), during which Angus claims to want to publish *Confession* because it is in demand. He wants Fay to find Henry's journals for publication, and he also asks her out on a date. While talking with Fay, Angus mentions Simon's trial five years earlier, and the film cuts to a flashback of their shared recollection of it.

Fay finally arrives at home to find two CIA agents, Fulbright (Jeff Goldblum) and Carl Fogg (Leo Fitzpatrick), who inquire about Henry's journals and present her with new evidence about his escape. They ask if she knows the name Bebe Konchalovsky and wonder if she has read

Figure 15: Fay (Parker Posey) examines Ned's (Liam Aiken) pornographic toy, which displays an orgy motion-picture loop that is never seen by viewers in *Fay Grim*.

the treasonous memoir (she says that she read only the "dirty parts") before they reveal that Henry never arrived in Sweden and that he is dead—a "fact" that some characters doubt, including Simon.

Simon believes that Henry's memoir is "too completely awful to be true" and must therefore actually be something else, so he enlists Angus in a plan to retrieve Henry's eight journals. Angus enlists Fay in the plan without revealing what he and Simon suspect, and soon after, a former CIA encryption expert (J. E. Heys) serving prison time with Simon examines one journal ("Book Six") and offers that Henry has played a role in international intrigue since at least 1973. The CIA agents loosely confirm some of this and ask Fay to retrieve two of Henry's notebooks from France before the French use them to blackmail the United States. She agrees to do so in exchange for Simon's release.

During her stay in France, Fay is tracked by competing spies and meets Bebe (Elina Löwensohn)—flight attendant, occasional topless dancer, and rumored Chechen rebel. Bebe narrates the film's second flashback—in which she mistakes Henry for "the great Simon Grim"—to explain how she helped Henry elude authorities in Sweden. Bebe and Henry have sex in the airplane bathroom, and she secretly escorts him off of the plane because Henry-as-Simon wants to escape his celebrity. The two drive to Berlin, and after more raucous sex, Bebe steals Henry's *Confession*, believing it to be Simon's new poems. She sells it to a Parisian drug dealer (Jef Bayonne), only to learn Henry's identity later when he finds her working in a Hamburg strip club.

Bebe is the catalyst for Fay's quest, since she scatters the journals. Once they meet, they form a team of women in love with Henry and follow his trail to Istanbul, leading Simon and various agents to the same locale. There, Henry resurfaces alive as the "guest-prisoner" of Jallal Said Khan (Anatole Taubman), a former garbageman from Kandahar, Afghanistan, a lookalike for Osama Bin Laden, and, in Fulbright's words, a "superstar mujahadeen" who considers Henry to be a mentor. Henry's relationship with Jallal predates his relationship with Simon, and he inspired Jallal to write a manifesto that Afghani authorities deemed pornographic before they imprisoned him. Jallal now needs to sever ties with Henry because his mentor's fame—as a possible spy and/or in relation to Simon's fame—will attract unwanted attention.

Jallal gives Fay Henry's final notebook, reveals that he sent the toy to

Ned to draw the family to find Henry, and spells out an escape plan via boat for Fay and Henry. As in *Henry Fool* and some of Hartley's other films, *Fay Grim* speeds toward its conclusion with choppy scenes: a suicide bomber sent by Jallal blows up the authorities who pursue Fay, including Fulbright; the police mistakenly shoot Bebe; Henry retrieves the eight notebooks from Simon; and Fay fails to save Bebe and arrives at the dock too late to meet Henry. Henry steams away on the boat with his journals before the film cuts to its final close-up shot of Fay looking toward Henry, while offscreen sirens and a gun being cocked indicate that the police have caught up with her.

| | |

As in Hartley's other films, *Fay Grim*'s plots accumulate in an absurdist fashion, and the deliberately hard-to-follow plotlines parallel Henry's own misdirection in the earlier film. Hartley's strategy of narrative obfuscation in this film undermines basic narrative intelligibility as a realist norm and opens up questions about Henry's earlier apparent misdirection, as odd bits of new information about him crop up.

It appears that Henry used a CIA code to write *Confession,* and *Paradise Lost* is its concordance throughout the eight volumes, a feat that could only be done intelligibly by a "savant" for a line or two. He might be or might have been an operative for the United States, a double agent for unknown forces, or a janitor who became a spy in South and Central America, Romania, Hungary, and/or Afghanistan. Henry could be a wannabe librarian or an actual chemist. No one is certain of his age, and given his unhealthy lifestyle, Simon speculates that he could be a "ravaged man in his thirties" or a "well-preserved fifty-year-old." Agents from the United States, France, Israel, an Israeli splinter group, Russia, North Korea, Germany, Belgium, China, Great Britain, Turkey, Saudi Arabia, and at least one Islamic group pursue Fay because they believe that Henry's notebooks are cover documents for all sorts of clandestine material. "Book One" might contain satellite coordinates, "Book Six" mentions a South American coup and Henry's relationship with Fulbright, while other notebooks are thought to be decoys. Elements such as these revise key details from *Henry Fool,* and we appreciate the contrast to be a critical consideration of realism's association with accurate information, comprehension, and stable knowledge.

The second film includes altered cinematography and a stylized mise-en-scène that depart from Hartley's usual palette to construct tensions about characters' (and our) established knowledge about Henry. Within the terrain established by Hartley's revised mise-en-scène and cinematography, a tripartite narrative introduces new information—Fay's global travels; the investigation of Henry conducted by Simon, Angus, and Ned in New York to aid Fay; and Fulbright's revelations about his shared past with Henry. These threads compete with the formerly held belief that Henry spread falsehoods about himself, an interpretation rooted within the first film's narrative logic.

Fay Grim's epistemological tension begins in the first scenes, where Fay is shown in a distinct alteration of Hartley's clean cinematic look. Hartley presents Fay in blurred, jump-cut exterior still shots that are intercut with his standard white-text-on-black-screen credits to suggest movement, a technique that he repeats at other moments in the film. When we are able to see Fay's face, she displays confused, lost, or searching expressions. Once the film is "in motion" in Fay's opening meetings, we begin to follow her madcap global adventure in search of Henry's notebooks. In these meetings, we cannot fail to notice that *Fay Grim* includes a sustained alteration of Hartley's cinematographic style: virtually every shot is canted so that most horizontal lines, such as doorways, window frames, furniture, and the exteriors of buildings, are shown to be off-kilter even when the foreground images appear to be level.

Canted angles do appear at discrete moments in *Henry Fool,* and Hartley says that the technique was used in these instances "to get that excitement you get in a documentary, but without sacrificing the evidence of formal construction. I didn't want it to be sloppy—I wanted the images to have a strong narrative voice. By using strong, intense angles, I was trying for the clarity of style I admire in comic books, and which is more about looking than showing" (Fuller, "Responding to Nature," xxii). This "more about looking than showing" effect is greatly amplified in *Fay Grim,* which of Hartley's films is the most reminiscent of comic books in terms of visual style and narrative progression. Hartley also refers to Fay as becoming a sort of superhero once she dons the trench coat that Angus gives her (figure 16). The film's angularity recalls comic-book frames at moments and conveys a skewed tone that guides our viewing. With this tonal consistency, we work through the jumble of episodic action in a rapid fashion, as we might with a comic book. We comprehend its general narrative thrust; we "get" its mood and perspective without drawing together each episode and detail in a coherent manner.

At the same time, the canted angles function as markers of space that do not designate the locale per se but rather connote the tone and the narrative context of the shots. The angles are a different take on establishing shots, which Hartley usually eschews in their typical format, to evoke an uncertain atmosphere that hangs over the actions and the relationships depicted within locales. A more traditional riff on establishing shots that extends narrative obfuscation is the use of superimposed titles that specify times and places over the canted angle shots. The titles assist in making sense of the unwieldy, multiple locations and timelines through their naming function, yet their execution also interrupts this clarity, since their placement obscures the images. The titles spread over much of the frame in different font sizes and in different directions, effectively modifying a specific Brechtian strategy of estrangement, what Jameson has described as moments in Brecht's theatrical practice when "titles dropped out of catwalk[s]" (*Brecht and Method,* 44–45). We know where we are in time and space, but this knowledge does not always yield comprehension.

Figure 16: Fay as a superhero on the streets of Paris in *Fay Grim*.

The divergent relationship between possession and comprehension of knowledge is a crucial element in the film that is highlighted by the contrast between the New York team's investigation and Fulbright's revelations about Henry. Simon, Angus, and Ned's investigation into the pornographic toy includes a ribald cinematic staging of a corny "a priest, a rabbi . . ." joke in several scenes. They show the toy to Father Lang so that he might translate the text that appears on the wall, as Angus clarifies, "behind the two girls with the goat." (A three-line title, "MEANWHILE / BACK HOME / THE WRITING ON THE WALL," is superimposed on the shot and alludes to the intertitles in *The Unbelievable Truth*.) Father Lang thinks it is Hebrew, but he "can't tell with all of the foreground debauchery." They next meet a rabbi (Tim Seyfi), who says that it is written in Arabic, which sends the group to meet an imam (Mehdi Nebbou), who recognizes the writing as Turkish and roughly translates it into what Simon rephrases as, "An honest man is always in trouble." He recognizes this line as Henry's motto and the first line of *Confession*. Just as we never hear Simon's poems or Henry's memoir, we never see the images and must rely on the characters' descriptions.

The conclusion of this investigation convinces Simon that Henry is in Turkey, which leads him to instruct Fay via a coded telephone call to go there. She understands Simon in a satisfactory conclusion of the toy investigation in which we see a rather straightforward, uncomplicated connection between knowledge and comprehension. Simon and his crew draw clues from the toy to deduce correctly Henry's location. In a similar fashion, we might guess the toy's connection to Henry before this, since Fay holds it in an early omniscient close-up shot that highlights the calligraphy on its top as the upside-down initials, "H.F."[11]

Comprehension of Fulbright's knowledge about Henry is not as simple, however, because Fulbright is an unreliable narrator, a characterization that aligns him with the view of Henry developed in the first film. Fulbright masks his real goal throughout the film, but his main interest finally seems to be the arrest or assassination of Jallal. Fay and Henry are collateral damage in Fulbright's pursuit of Jallal, and he reluctantly reveals conflicting information about Henry when it might advance this pursuit. He tells Fay that Henry's journals are a forced confession from when Henry was captured in Chile in 1973, but in a later scene, announced by a superimposed title as "Fulbright's Confession," Fulbright tells Fogg, Angus, Ned, and Simon that he concocted a forgery of Henry's 1973 confession without knowing if he actually wrote a confession. The provenance of Henry's journals has become more confused since the Russians, British, Chinese, Pakistanis, and Germans used or created their own forgeries and translations.[12]

Simon (in the spirit of Michel Foucault and Roland Barthes) names Henry's "masterpiece . . . a collection of fakes of a book that has never itself been written," while Angus calls it a "self-perpetuating literature of obfuscation, hearsay, rumor, innuendo, and outright lies. A bestseller for sure." Fulbright offers a third assessment and names the journals—or, rather, the multiple versions of them—"fucking psychological terrorism," which leads into his flashback, titled "Afghanistan 1989." Fulbright speaks with another spy, Andre, about the United States backing Jallal as a leader and learns that Henry mentors Jallal. Jallal's story mirrors Simon's, and Fulbright corroborates that Henry has had some involvement in international geopolitics, but the flashback does not help explain the journals' value, which edition Henry actually possesses, nor whether Henry actually wrote a confession in 1973. Is Fulbright the "author" who has produced the source material for Henry's fame, which in turn inspires Jallal and Simon to write and make their own celebrity?

In *The Unbelievable Truth, Simple Men,* and *Amateur,* Hartley presents revised or competing views of the past to challenge characters' "secure knowledge" about others—Josh is a bad man, Mr. McCabe is a bomber, Kate's ex-husband is an unrepentant abuser, and Thomas cannot alter his identity. These supposed facts are called into question as impressionistic recollections or outright fabrications eventually, and in *Fay Grim,* Hartley offers his most elaborate version of this narrative thematic extended over two films. Henry has had an intrigue-filled life and is no longer thought to be a liar as he was in *Henry Fool,* although when he does appear in *Fay Grim,* he still is a loudmouthed buffoon. Yet even this revision of his character cannot stand, since Fulbright's knowledge of Henry tweaks the revision and suggests that he is a plagiarist. Henry has been in the hotspot locales, but in what capacity? The *actual* interest in his journals signals that there might be some truth contained within them, but is Henry their author? The second film does not answer these questions but instead reverts to a character trait of Henry's that remains consistent with the first film. He again leaves Fay and Simon behind to negotiate the fallout from his offenses, while he escapes all punishment and responsibility. Fay's unsettled conclusion thus gives rise to a rather ominous predicament in which she is punished for the misdeeds of another, at least until the next installment.

The Apocalypse, Digitized

The Book of Life

The Book of Life is the U.S. entry into the multi-film 2000 *Seen By* series about the new millennium (see Durbin). Hartley's innovative variation on Christian conceptions of the Apocalypse and the Second Coming of Jesus provide the template for the film, with Jesus (Martin Donovan) returned to earth to judge the living and the dead at the end of the world. Like so many of Hartley's characters, Jesus has questions about the direction of his life and is conflicted about his role in the Apocalypse.

Hartley departs from his more common dialogue-driven narration to structure *The Book of Life*'s loose images with Jesus's first-person voiceover. *The Girl from Monday* also uses a protagonist's voiceover, and *No Such Thing* includes moments of voiceover in the form of the protagonist writing letters to her dead fiancé; these are the few instances of voiceovers in Hartley's films. Jesus first appears accompanied by his associate, Magdalena (P. J. Harvey), as they meet a troubled white man (James Urbaniak) at a New York airport. This man, listed as "True Believer" in the final credits, repeats, "Forgive me, Jesus, for I have sinned. Have mercy on us now and at the hour of our death," while the camera moves erratically to follow his movements. When he touches and calms the man, we hear Jesus say in voiceover, "Mercy. I could never get used to that part of the job."

The voiceover continues with significant pauses over credit shots, shots of Jesus and Magdalena hailing a cab and riding in it through the city: "The power and the glory, the threat of divine vengeance. But I persevered. I was about my father's business, and I was a good son. It was the morning of December 31, 1999, when I returned at last to judge the living and the dead, though still and perhaps always, I had my doubts."

Donovan-as-Jesus wears a placid expression, not unlike Thomas's vacant expressions in *Amateur*. Donovan's casting in both roles provides an intertextual link between both characters' rather complicated resurrections. From the airport, they check into a hotel whose logo is an angel holding a sword and begin their retrieval of the Book of Life, the central text of the Apocalypse. A hotel safe-deposit box holds a key that opens up locker 666 at a bowling alley, where they find the Book of Life, a late-1990s Macintosh Powerbook. We should remember that when *The Book of Life* was produced, real trepidation about the Y2K-induced computer collapse at the new millennium did exist, which for some meant a possible technological apocalypse and for others a time of divine reckoning. Such fears are called up in the use of the Macintosh.

Satan (Thomas Jay Ryan) stalks Jesus and Magdalena at the hotel and throughout their quest, and in a clever way, Hartley's casting of Ryan as the Devil extratextually fulfills some of *Henry Fool*'s depiction of Henry as a demon. Save his costume, Ryan appears exactly as he did in *Henry Fool* and plays both characters as acerbic, slightly clownish lushes. In discussing Henry, Hartley gives an early indication as to how he will characterize Satan in *The Book of Life*: "There's the idea that the Devil was once an angel, too, but he's on the outs with the front office. I've always believed that the Devil has a place in our Western Judeo-Christian sense of morality. Andrew Delbanco has written in *The Death of Satan* how one of the problems of Western society now is that we've lost our appreciation of what the Devil is: he's not scary any more. Yet I think the Devil of Christian mythology serves a real purpose. As the unseen haphazard cause of things, he symbolizes anarchy" (Fuller, "Responding to Nature," xiv).

While Jesus and Satan battle, the film's entertaining subplots beg for more sustained attention as Jesus deliberates his role in the Apocalypse. A scheming, self-interested white lawyer (D. J. Mendel) sports a waxed, villain's handlebar moustache and works at "Armageddon, Armageddon, and Jehoshaphat," God's law firm, with his blonde, quick-witted assistant (Katreen Hardt). Jesus notes that his father "is an angry god" who loves lawyers because "to him the law is everything," and the lawyer attempts to carry out God's plan in unorthodox ways: he detains and questions Magdalena, berates Jesus, and has a shootout with two Mormons (Paul Albe and Don Creech).

Another subplot follows Dave (Dave Simonds), a white disheveled gambling addict and denizen of the hotel's bar where his near-saintly, "terminally-good" Japanese girlfriend Edie (Miho Nikaido) works. Dave is on a losing streak, and Edie wants to take care of him and serve vegetarian soup to the homeless. Satan tempts Dave when he asks if he would bargain Edie's soul to become a winner. Dave responds, "Take a powder, creep," but soon inadvertently gambles away Edie's soul when he buys a winning lottery ticket with Satan's money. The money allows Edie to make and distribute soup, and when Dave figures out what has happened, he explains to Magdalena that he did not know that he was gambling Edie's soul because he is an atheist.

Dave's mistake prompts Jesus to trade the Book of Life with Satan for Edie's soul. Satan, however, cannot open the Book of Life, and he stumbles about the city looking for help. He meets God's lawyer and assistant, who attempts to broker a deal with Satan, who responds by asking his assistant out and escorting her back to the hotel, where, rather bizarrely, Satan and the assistant join Jesus, Magdalena, Edie, and Dave for a fun-loving New Year's Eve party. At the party, Jesus surreptitiously reclaims the Book of Life from Satan.

Abstract shots fill out the remainder of the film: blurred and jerky images of New York City streets; skaters on an ice rink; the hotel party; black-and-white shots of a Salvation Army band (played by Yo La Tengo) playing a dirge; and "morning after" shots of the partygoers riding a ferry out of New York City. We hear a heavily layered sound track in these shots that consists of diegetic laughter; the Salvation Army band's diegetic music; the nondiegetic "Love Too Soon," a song by Pascal Comelade and P. J. Harvey; and Jesus's long final voiceover. The final wide shot shows him standing with his back toward the camera on the ferry's deck (similar to Henry's departure in *Fay Grim*), and the shot is lit in a slightly hazy, gray, pink, and yellow scheme as the sun rises behind the skyline, including the prominent World Trade Center (figure 17). With little flourish, Jesus heaves the Book of Life into the ferry's wake before his voiceover concludes the film.

| | |

The Book of Life represents an aesthetic break from Hartley's other work, a break that is even more pronounced than the canted angles

Figure 17: The concluding image of
The Book of Life, with the World Trade
Center in the background as Jesus (Martin
Donovan) prepares to throw the Book
of Life laptop into the ferry's wake.

and still images of the later *Fay Grim. The Book of Life* is Hartley's first feature-length digital-video production, which in part accounts for the shakeup of his usual cinematography and mise-en-scène. It was Hartley's first feature-length film not to employ his longtime collaborator Michael Spiller as cinematographer. Hartley and the cinematographer Jim Denault explored digital special-effects in *The Book of Life* to create a generally blurred, moving-camera style that contrasts with the much more static, "clean," filmic-photographic visual style for which Hartley is known. The film similarly presents much less precise editing so that it has an overall loose feel when looked at alongside Hartley's other work.

There is no mistaking that *The Book of Life* is shot on digital video, while in comparison, *Fay Grim* uses HDCAM digital video to present a far more filmic style that builds upon Hartley's signature look.[13] In an interview about *The Girl from Monday* with *GreenCine* that was conducted before Hartley shot *Fay Grim,* Hartley offers his thoughts about the distinctions between digital video, film stock (what he calls "motion picture photography"), and HD:

I was never attracted to video as a substitute for motion picture photography. I love motion picture photography. . . . I like video, too. I try to look for qualities I can get out of digital video that are endemic to it, rather than just trying to cop the look of motion pictures. HD is a different thing. My next movie [*Fay Grim*] will probably be in high definition video. Then I don't really see any appreciable difference between motion picture photography and HD. The resolution is just tremendous. When I work in video, I like to say that I do damage to the camera. I spent months making shorter pieces to try and figure out when the camera [the Sony VX2000 in *The Girl From Monday*] freaks out. . . . I've always thought of it as the visual equivalent of what electronic popular music or amplified electric music has been making for fifteen years now. Distortion has a visual texture. I'm apt to be listening to Sonic Youth more as a reference than I am watching movies, because there's much more freedom in music about using distortion. All that blurriness comes out of that aesthetic. (Eaves)

In *Higher Definition with Robert Wilonsky,* Hartley confirms that shooting in HD did turn out to be like shooting on thirty-five millimeter. Following from Hartley's description of what is endemic to digital video and his comparison of visual blurriness to distortion in amplified electric music, we see that the aesthetic logic of *The Book of Life* offers us a busy visual experience: onscreen lights, reflective surfaces, and windows create lens flares; bleary light bleeds occur throughout; onscreen movements blur into out-of-focus action or appear in jerky clips where actors are not recognizable; black-and-white images are cut into color scenes; and the use of available, ambient light distorts color to cast images in green, blue, and red hues that resemble the cross-processing of film stock. In addition to these digital elements, the extensive use of a handheld camera and some canted angles, techniques not unique to digital video, augment the digital-video aesthetic. Again, *Fay Grim* makes more use of canted angles, but not in a manner that highlights its status as video.

Along with this digital style, *The Book of Life*'s mise-en-scène is playful in its revision of biblical elements—the urban setting, the Powerbook. Jesus dresses in a rather plain, medium-blue suit, a white shirt, and a maroon tie, while Magdalena is far more stylish in her all-black ensemble of a coat, a low-cut blouse, a choker, and tight leather pants; with her blunt bangs, Magdalena virtually reproduces Sofia's style from *Amateur* and presents a precise visual link between the biblical former prostitute and the famous porn star. Here, Jesus's and Magdalena's costumes and the casting of the well-known rock musician P. J. Harvey creates a compelling dissonance between the two characters that will be maintained throughout the film—Jesus *looks like* an accountant or a midlevel sales representative, and Magdalena *is* a rock star (figure 18). Unlike the neat Jesus, Satan appears as a white man with greasy, brown, chin-length hair, a five o'clock shadow, an unexplained black eye, and a band-aid on his brow; he wears a black suit, a thin black necktie, and, of course, a blood-red shirt. He gets his own theme song, an instrumental rhythm-and-blues song that brings to mind a blaxploitation soundtrack in the vein of Isaac Hayes's "Theme from *Shaft*," which suddenly cuts in and out whenever Satan appears.

Set against Jesus's accountant style, however, is his voiceover, which is presented in the style of film-noir narration that befits the film's urban setting. In "*Film Noir,* Voice-Over, and the Femme Fatale," Karen Hollinger writes that the genre's "use of [the] first person voice-over . . . commonly involves a confessional/investigational mode [that] penetrates

Figure 18: Jesus the accountant with Magdalena (P. J. Harvey) the rock star in their hotel room in *The Book of Life.*

into . . . a character's psyche in order to arrive at a fundamental truth [about the individual's] socially abnormal or destructive situation" (244), a description that fits Jesus's plight in *The Book of Life.* Hartley's use of the voiceover creates a disjuncture between genre convention and the pious associations about Jesus, as it presents a film-noir antihero trapped by a social structure, not a man-god who is an agent within his life. No stranger to confession, Jesus expresses a deep internal conflict about his role in his father's plan, just as some noir protagonists become implicated in the cases they investigate.

For some, Jesus ought to be the agent of divine reckoning, but in Hartley's worldview he is a character who fears apocalyptic change as much as humans do. He also is a child engaged in an Oedipal conflict with his (absent) father, like so many of Hartley's protagonists. Hartley clearly situates Jesus as a character within the contemporary, everyday social world—he still has to fly on an airplane, take a taxicab, and stay at a hotel—so as god-made flesh, he is in an abnormal situation. And no destructive situation can surpass *the* Apocalypse. Along with the voiceover's noir pedigree, *The Book of Life* makes use of common noir locations such as urban streets, offices, hotels, and bars, where transient characters pursue each other, engage in conspiracy, and drink alcohol constantly (see Sobchack).

Satan is an obvious counterpoint to Jesus, and one way that Hartley amplifies their conflict is to set Jesus's voiceover against Satan's monologue asides. Satan delivers these monologues at three moments in the film, and Hartley depicts them with direct-address shots and an onscreen microphone placed on a stand. Similar onscreen microphone techniques are used in *No Such Thing,* when the Monster (Robert John Burke) speaks to viewers, and throughout Hartley's play *Soon.*

Satan's first monologue takes place in a restroom at the hotel just after he tempts Dave. He stands in front of the restroom sink in a cramped medium shot, and the conjunction of two mirrors placed at a right angle causes him to appear in triplicate (figure 19). Satan has his back to the camera, so we see his direct address and the microphone most clearly in reflection when he speaks about his attempt to steal Edie's soul: "Sure, go ahead, call me petty, but one more good soul snatched away from the all-knowing unknowable is still another feather in my cap. So what if it's the last day of the world? I'm not going to give in without a fight, come what may. Let God the almighty rule eternity. My precincts are the minutes and the hours of the everyday. And as long as people have hopes and dreams, well then, I'll have my work to do."

When Jesus and Satan do meet to converse, the voiceover/monologue conflict is suspended in a comical version of Satan's biblical temptation of Jesus, reset within the stylized locale of a subterranean Russian-themed bar. Jesus approaches a banquette, where an aggravated Satan yells, "This is breaking the rules, you know!" Jesus sits and sums up his feelings: he doesn't want to judge the living and the dead because "this divine vengeance crap is all wrong," too "exclusive." Although Satan does not know it, Jesus has already thrown the Book of Life into a trashcan on the street, but Magdalena has retrieved it, unbeknownst to him. The two drink vodka shots as their quick-paced conversation advances in Hartley's absurdist style, cut between oddly framed shots that at moments place Satan behind Jesus as a life-sized devil-on-one's-shoulder. Satan accuses Jesus of fomenting revolution because Jesus believes that he and Satan have "allowed a huge misunderstanding to distort the soul of humanity." They agree that humans created them, and Satan asserts that "people just like to kill each other" and that Jesus, attracted to the "allure of [humans'] free will, [is] addicted to human beings."

Figure 19: One of Satan's (Thomas Jay Ryan)
monologues in *The Book of Life.*

As an endgame, Satan attempts to convince Jesus that they should start a new religion, but Jesus refuses and walks out of the bar. Satan yells, "You can never go home again! That's it! We're in the same boat now, you and me. Sink or swim! You're a man without a country, an exile," and the film cuts to the final shot at the bar, an exterior shot of Jesus walking up the bar's exterior stairs to the street level. Satan follows to confront him about the location of the Book of Life, and Jesus's wordless response is to punch Satan in the stomach in the overdone, comic manner common to Hartley's representation of physical fights.

With Jesus's departure, his voiceover reenters the film. He admits that Satan is right, because "nothing ever changes and no one ever learns." Although Jesus claims that nothing ever changes, the bar scene enacts quite the opposite. Everything has changed—unlike the usual biblical stories about Jesus's doubts and temptations, this scene represents his rejection of his father's plan and his fall from grace, a fall that is marked aurally when Satan's theme song plays over Jesus's later actions. As Satan observes, Jesus has become a heretic, a revolutionary, and one of the fallen as the result of his own agency, and the real temptation comes from humans themselves—or, as Satan names it, from an addiction to them. It seems that Jesus wants to save humans because he desires them, and it is this matter of desire that brings us back to Magdalena.

While Jesus's addiction to humans is explicit in *The Book of Life,* his particular desire for the once human and now seemingly immortal Magdalena is not. Do Magdalena and Jesus travel together as employer and assistant, as lovers, or as something else? They share a hotel room as "Mr. and Mrs. D. W. Griffith," an allusion to another film director who has depicted Jesus's trials, and they are shown resting together in an intimate position on a hotel bed. When we hear directly from Magdalena, however, it seems that Jesus overlooks her affection, while she announces her longing for him.

A few scenes highlight Magdalena's love for Jesus, first when she travels to Armageddon, Armageddon, and Jehoshaphat and is grilled by the lawyer about the Book of Life's whereabouts. The overwhelming red and yellow "hot" tone of the lighting creates the feeling of an interrogation, but Magdalena conceals what she knows and tells the lawyer that Jesus is "willing to forgive, completely." Later in the scene, Magdalena recounts the first time she met Jesus, when he defended her from a crowd about to stone her, even after the crowd told him "what [she] was." When the assistant, who takes notes in a stenographer notepad, asks, "And what were you?" the lawyer responds in a flat tone, "Adulteress. Whore. Prostitute," to which the assistant responds, "Self-employed." The lawyer then gets a telephone call and announces "new developments" that allow Magdalena to leave, but she concludes her story with, "I thought he'd fallen in love with me." The assistant commiserates by saying, "He's that kind of guy," before the film cuts to Magdalena's exit, a close-up that reframes into a wide shot and overexposes into blinding white light.

We see a series of jump-cut, handheld close-ups soon after of Magdalena inside a record store, where she listens to music at a listening station and dances. We do not hear what she listens to but instead hear her belt out snippets from Lulu's pop song "To Sir, with Love" (figure 20). With the "Sir" in this situation surely Jesus, Magdalena's performance plays with the original context of the song and announces her desire for an (unattainable) authority figure, in this case her "boss" rather than a teacher. Hartley complicates Harvey's performance with the addition of a second song to the sound track, her heavy industrial "The Faster I Breathe, the Further I Go," so that our aural experience is to hear Harvey layered in two noncomplementary tracks that compete for our attention. A "listening" of this scene might allow us to appreciate Magdalena's split, unrequited love experience; even with her rock-star persona, Magdalena will never overcome the distance or the authority dynamic between her and Jesus.

No clear resolution to Magdalena's dilemma is shown in the film, but her desire for Jesus again crops up as she, Edie, Dave, and Satan lounge in a hotel room and wait for Jesus. Satan seizes upon Magdalena's love for Jesus and mocks her by calling him her "boyfriend," to which an annoyed Magdalena replies, "You're so unimaginative." Before more can be made of this, Jesus arrives and exchanges the Book of Life for Edie's soul, leading into the film's New Year conclusion, which is dominated by Jesus's final voiceover:

And the New Year arrived. The new millennium. Just another day in a lifetime of similar days, but each one of them crowded with possibilities. The possibility of disaster and the possibility of perfection. To be there amongst them again was good. The innocent and the guilty all equally helpless, all perfectly lost, and, as frightening as it was to admit,

Figure 20: Magdalena's energetic performance
of "To Sir, with Love," in a New York City
record store in *The Book of Life.*

all deserving of forgiveness. What would become of them, I wonder? In another hundred years, would they all be born in test tubes? Or perhaps evolve through computers to become groups of disembodied digital intelligence machines? Would they remember who I was? Would they remember what I said? Would it matter? Maybe someone else will come along and say pretty much the same thing. Would anyone notice? In a hundred years, would they be living on other planets? Would the earth still exist? Would they engineer themselves genetically so that disease was a thing of the past? Would they all just become one big multiethnic race? Would they discover the secret of the universe? God? Would they become gods themselves? What will they eat? What sort of houses will they live in? Cities? Think about it. What will the weather be like? Will they still have to go to work everyday? What will they wear in the future? How smart will they get? And will being smarter make them happier? Will they all speak the same language in the future? Will they make love? Maybe there will be more than two sexes. Will they still think that life is sacred? Will it matter? Do we matter?

The futurity of Jesus's voiceover is striking, since it seems to suggest that he will not survive to see the future. Indeed, "the" future as a singular, prophesized event has been replaced by "a lifetime of similar days . . . each one of them crowded with possibilities" in which no single, predetermined reality structures existence. No longer immortal, Jesus wonders if he matters, then if we matter, a verbal signal that his desire for and addiction to humans has resulted in his transformation into one. For the moment, this transformation radically alters Jesus's own future—he will not survive or perhaps even be remembered, even if the world persists.

Conclusion

To return to the opening and ongoing concept of escape in Hartley's work, we might consider the conjunction of extrafilmic elements and *The Book of Life*'s conclusion as a metaphor for the director's own trajectory after 2001. Jesus's departure from New York prefigures Hartley's departure from the city and its suburbs when he moved to Berlin in 2005. This move, which Hartley has indicated has at least some relationship to the aftermath of September 11 (see Avila's interview with Hartley in this volume), is not as dramatic as Jesus's departure or as the escapes that many of his other characters enact, yet it is notable for a director whose work has been so thoroughly associated with aspects of life in the United States. Just as the end of the Long Island era extended Hartley's creative interests into new aesthetic and narrative directions, his most recent relocation will likely present another extension of his work, as is already evident in the global scope of *Fay Grim*. While some of Hartley's probing representations remain consistent with his earliest work—what it means to have integrity, to trust another person, and to resist exploitation and objectification—his characters struggle within new terrain as they confront social mores, surveillance, policing, and violence, which have come to represent a troubling contemporary context. Hartley, of course, could not know in 1998 how *The Book of Life*'s conclusion would resonate after September 11, 2001, yet the final image, including the World Trade Center in the New York skyline along with Jesus's remarks about the "possibility of disaster," create an eerie tone. The fictive becomes blurry, since Jesus's role as a god on earth and the cityscape shown no longer exist. He avoided disaster, but the city did not.

Notes

1. I do not use the term "antirealism" to be synonymous with countercinema, a term associated with Godard that describes a more radical and more overtly leftist political cinema. Some sense of kinship between the two directors led Hartley to interview Godard for *Filmmaker* magazine in 1994 (Godard, "In Images We Trust"); on this exchange, see Robert Avila's interview with Hartley in this volume. An enigmatic character (Nick Gomez) in the 1991 short *Theory of Achievement* is modeled on Godard, and clips of an interview with Godard appear in Hartley's short *Accomplice* (2009). Also see Hartley, *True Fiction Pictures and Possible Films;* Fuller, "Finding the Essential" and "Responding to Nature"; Canby, "Mismatched Brothers on a Godardian Road"; Hartley, "Interview with Hal Hartley"; and Bordwell, "Up Close and Impersonal."

2. On politics in Hartley's films, see Wood, *Pocket Essentials*, 111; Fuller, "Finding the Essential," xxv. On Brecht, see Fuller, "Being an Amateur," xxxix.

3. On Hartley and Jarmusch, see Deer, "Hal Hartley"; and Wood, *Pocket Essentials*, 114.

4. See Andersen, "Finding the Essential"; Fuller, "Finding the Essential," xxiv; Wood, *Pocket Essentials*, 115. On humor, see Fried, "Rise of an Indie"; and the documentary *Professional Amateurs.*

5. On independent film, see Andrew, *Stranger Than Paradise*; Hillier, *American Independent Cinema*; Holmlund and Wyatt, *Contemporary American Independent Film*; King, *American Independent Cinema*; Levy, *Cinema of Outsiders*; Lewis, *New American Cinema*; Man, *Radical Visions*; and Suárez, *Jim Jarmusch.* On Hartley's thoughts about the term "independent," see Hartley and Kaleta, *True Fiction Pictures and Possible Films*; Hartley, "indieWIRE Interview"; and Justin Wyatt's interview with Hartley in this volume.

6. A similar running joke appears in John Ford's *Stagecoach* (1939), where the drunk Doc Boone (Thomas Mitchell) consistently misrecognizes the "whiskey drummer" Peacock (Donald Meek) as a preacher because Peacock is dressed in all black and carries a black satchel.

7. Hartley plans out the choreography, the geometry of camera setups, and general blocking in schematic diagrams designed with his cinematographers, as opposed to the more common practice of creating storyboards. *The Making of Fay Grim; or, How Do You Spell Espionage?* includes several moments that superimpose the diagrams over shots from the corresponding scenes from the final film. Also see Fuller, "Finding the Essential"; and Comer, "*Amateur's* Tenebrous Images."

8. For Hartley's thoughts on this scene, see Fuller, "Being an Amateur," xl–xli. Kurt is startled by Isabelle and Thomas at Sofia's apartment before this, and he falls through a window in a repetition of Thomas's unseen fall.

9. Simon sees his mother play the piano in one earlier scene, but she stops and says that her efforts are "unremarkable," which is the spark for his initiative with

Angus. Hartley imagines that in Mrs. Grim's back story, she had "once shown some promise as a pianist [but then] got knocked up in high school while she was waiting to get into music school, and then her boyfriend was drafted and got killed [in Vietnam], so she got stuck with these kids—something mundanely tragic like that" (Fuller, "Responding to Nature," xvi).

10. See Godard, "In Images We Trust," for a brief account of Hartley's thoughts on this phenomenon in relation to film distribution in 1994.

11. Fay reads the initials late in the film in Istanbul, when a concierge (Erdal Yildiz) identifies them as a sign of the historic "Harem Fool" figure, not Henry Fool, although the distinction might not matter. The concierge sends Fay to a shop that sells the toys, where she meets a blind middleman (Adnan Maral) for Jallal, who sends her to his secret location.

12. Untrustworthy characters like Henry and Fulbright abound in the film: Andre (Harald Schrott) is an Iranian in the employ of Russia working as double agent against the United States; Juliet (Saffron Burrows) is a double agent spying on the United States for the Israelis; Milla is Juliet's aid and Angus's assistant, who shoots Angus and tries to kill Ned; Fay's French liaison Picard (Peter Benedict) could be working against her; and an Arab operative named Amin (Nikolai Kinski) asks for Fay's help but dies with the promise that his group will destroy the United States.

13. Sarah Cawley (Cabiya) shot *Fay Grim* on HDCAM digital video format, making it Hartley's third feature-length film to originate on a nonfilmic format. Cawley also shot Hartley's short film *Kimono* (2000) and *The Girl from Monday* and was the first assistant camera on *The Unbelievable Truth* and *Trust*.

"The Particularity and Peculiarity of Hal Hartley: An Interview"

Interview by Justin Wyatt, 1997. Originally published in *Film Quarterly*, Vol. 52, Number 1, Fall 1998 (University of California Press).

JUSTIN WYATT: While all of your films alternate between comic and serious moments, the tone seems to have become much darker with *Henry Fool*.

HAL HARTLEY: The tone may be a little more serious, but I don't really think that *Henry Fool* is a movie that posits a dark view of the world. I think that it offers an enormous amount of forgiveness and a lot of room for people who are different. In order to render that feeling, I did have to get into specifically dark situations. Henry, of course, is dark, but he's dark in the way that Mephistopheles is dark in *Faust*. He's a character who is a devil, but also foolish, funny, and witty.

JW: Were you concerned about the audience having to identify with Henry, who is, after all, completely dissolute, a pedophile, and a drunkard?

HH: I wanted people to identify with him because of the ugly parts, to recognize that a person at a particular place and time is capable of either making horrible mistakes or doing heroic deeds. What's really exciting for me as a reader or as a film viewer is the testing of my allegiance to a character. If I like somebody, and suddenly the text starts giving me clues that I'm being duped with the character—what happens? That emotional connection can be manipulated and toyed with.

I wanted a character who was completely perverted and dumb in certain simple ways but, at the same time, brilliant. He says a lot of great things which I pulled out of books along the way.

JW: Traditionally, your films seem based around a certain refusal to state certain things, to show certain things. . . .

HH: That's true. I remember that in *Amateur*, like most of my other films, a lot is not shown. I was more interested in what happens when people talk about something that happened in the past or something that will happen in the future or is simply happening somewhere else. There's something else going on: the immediate intimate maneuvering of people around each other while they are dealing with information. In the sea change that's been gradually happening with the work, that's one of the things that I began to notice and had an urge to do differently. I thought that I don't want them to talk about what is happening or will happen, I want to witness them doing; I want to look at the actual event. It's funny, I talk to other filmmakers, and they tell me, "Well, that's how we got into filmmaking in the first place. That was our first urge." My first urge was to watch the people conversing or struggling with each other about other things.

JW: Are you trying to break through this reserve that has been part of your style?

HH: It's liberating to break through that reserve. Of course, it was dictated by the story. I knew that I had written the story in a way to suggest an ugly, loud, and abrasive environment.

JW: *Henry Fool* is conceptualized on a grander scale than the other films and seems more committed to the lived experience of the characters.

HH: I wanted the characters to be more recognizable to general people. I don't think I had been so interested in that in the past—although in *Trust* and *The Unbelievable Truth*, perhaps so. In the other films, the particularity and the peculiarity of the people were enough for me. In this one, I really wanted more people to be able to recognize these characters and their problems. I wanted to leave a very specific impression of what it's like to live in America at this point in time. In terms of the scope, at a certain point in my work, I said I really want to tell a big fat story, a character-based story. That usually means recognition—we have to recognize these characters. That's the fun and the art of fiction, trying to take characters that are patently unbelievable and make them recognizable to us.

JW: Were there inspirations for this larger-scale enterprise?

HH: There's a lot of classical balance that I am striving for with *Henry Fool.* I was watching David Lean movies—*Lawrence of Arabia, Dr. Zhivago*—epic stories. Not just movies, though, I also looked to grand novels. That's what I was reaching for. The "Seven Years Later" [the final section of the film jumps ahead to explore the modified character relationships after this period of time] was absolutely essential from the very beginning. The movie had to be a little bit longer—it had to have the rhythm of a conclusion and then open up for another twenty minutes. I felt like I was taking part in a tradition.

I guess that I operate from an understanding that no matter what I'm trying to do, it's always going to come out being a Hal Hartley film, for lack of a better term. Yes, I'm looking at *Dr. Zhivago,* but I'm trying to tell this story about this guy living in Queens. What does that have to do with Russia and the Revolution? Well, nothing, but with storytelling, modes of telling stories, we don't really improve on them as time goes on. That doesn't mean that we shouldn't test the limits of a storytelling mode, try to find new ways of saying things.

JW: Do you conceive of an audience for your film?

HH: I think about the audience all the time. I populate my mind with a big room full of people who are more or less just like me. I don't even know if it's honest to say anything else. What do I know about other people, about what will entertain them? If I do more than that, then I am actually being calculating. The thing about calculation that I've always resisted is that there's an assumption being made that I know who you are, and I know what you think is important, what is funny, and what is moving. I really don't think that's true in life; I think that we're mysterious to each other, and that's one of the reasons, for instance, that we keep telling ourselves stories. Stories can be told and retold because we don't really know how we're going to react.

JW: One reading of *Henry Fool* is to interpret the film in terms of your understanding of the artistic process and also your place in the independent film world: Hartley as the individualistic Simon and the mainstream studio system as Henry Fool.

HH: That would be a stretch. I think that Henry and Simon are both aspects of me, and of any dynamic, artistic career. There's a lot of hot air that you must have when you go into the world and say, "I think my film's worth watching." It's frankly unbelievable, and when I was younger I never thought that I would have the gumption to say, "You all should stop what you're doing and pay attention to me."

That's countered by your talents often arising from your weaknesses and your misconceptions. Your own style is often the result of an inability to manipulate more conventional styles—you're getting something wrong, and it becomes your mode of working and conceptualizing. David Byrne once told me that he was trying to make a song sound like K. C. and the Sunshine Band—a dance thing—and he got it completely wrong and yet it became one of the more famous songs for the Talking Heads. I think that process happens a lot.

JW: You have been heralded as one of the most important voices in American independent cinema. To what extent do you feel that the label of "independent" is meaningful for you and your work?

HH: I really don't think much about the distinction between independents and Hollywood—or didn't until I was making *Trust*. Nick Gomez and I were in the editing room looking at head shots from people, and they were saying, "I like you indies!" And I remember distinctly saying, "What's an indie?" He said he didn't know, and, about two hours later, he said, "I think it means independent." It's a useful distinction at a certain point. I began using it from that day on—it does make some sense to me. I produce my movies independently. I do business independently. I never utilized it to signify an aesthetic difference, though. There have been plenty of films made in Hollywood that I liked: *Slaughterhouse-Five* was made by a studio, the Terrence

Malick films were studio pictures. The worst that I can say about Hollywood is that it tends to limit the amount of alternative work.

JW: You locate the difference between independent and mainstream primarily in commercial and industrial terms. Do you feel that aesthetic deviations grow from these larger structural ones?

HH: I think that they do. The business and aesthetics do go hand-in-hand. In 1993, it was really easy for me to get money to make *Simple Men* and then *Amateur*. Suddenly everything started homogenizing more and more . . . you would get approached by perfectly intelligent producers and distributors who might want to give you money, and a couple of years before they told me, "Okay, do your thing! I think it's going to make us money. If it's a sensible budget, it will be a great business deal for all of us." Just two years later, it was more like, "Don't do quite your thing. Can you do your thing but make it a little bit more like these movies that did business last year? . . . We have the figures right here." Then they bring out all these charts. I don't understand that. If the movie turns out to be a failure at the box office anyway, they would still think that I was the asshole, I didn't study the charts correctly. Whenever there's fear on the investor's part, I just say, "Give me less money. You're afraid to give me a million dollars, how about eight hundred thousand? Does that make you feel better? Do you feel less exposed?"

JW: Do you change the script to adjust for a lower amount of money?

HH: No, I don't change the script. I mean, I wrote *Henry Fool* thinking that I would make it for three million, which is still for most people very low budget, but it would have been big for me. I made it for about one million. I didn't change anything of substance; if I had more money, there would have been more crowd scenes, maybe. *Henry Fool* is the cheapest film for me since *Trust*. I spend 95 percent of my time raising financing and 5 percent making films. I have to worry about money constantly.

JW: Your films—from *Trust* through *Amateur* and *Henry Fool*—evidence a rather conflicted attitude toward technology and the corporate world. Does this reflect your own ambivalence to these arenas?

HH: I've never been particularly computer literate, and I have to become so. The thing I've decided to spend my life doing is becoming more and more digital and computerized. I don't want to be the kind of filmmaker who just has editors that do that work. For me, it must be hands-on. I take classes on computers and try to pick up what I can. I'm part owner of a digital editing facility, yet I still take night courses to learn how to work a Macintosh computer! As far as the corporate aspect goes, it's partly why I fear Hollywood: as the corporation becomes large, it becomes naturally less curious. With producing movies, this means that you'll start producing movies that are more certain of reaching a broad audience all the time. As my own company, True Fiction Pictures, gets bigger, I worry that I'll spend all my time managing the company and not working.

JW: There are always moments of the comic grotesque in your movies—Edward shooting Jan over and over in *Amateur*, the operation scenes in *Flirt*—and this is more pronounced in the new film.

HH: In this one, I just wanted the smell, the stink, and the ugliness to be right there. Self-expression, forgiveness, love to come up through a pile of garbage. It was a kind of good impatience: to look at the crud of life. My first impulse is to not look at, to turn away. What can I say . . . in this film, I even have a puking scene! Although to me, it's like Puke 101—a first-time student filmmaker's attempt at shock value.

JW: Are you concerned about your films straying too far to the side of self-consciousness and self-reflexivity?

HH: With *Henry Fool,* I didn't want to be too self-reflexive. It didn't seem appropriate. With *Amateur,* more so. *Flirt* is an essay about me making my work, as much as anything else.

JW: *Flirt,* to me, reveals you as an artist experimenting with the medium, yet still within the boundaries of commercial entertainment. Who else would you place in that category: filmmakers that teach you about storytelling and cinematic narration?

HH: Todd Haynes, Michael Almereyda, who made *Nadja,* Gregg Araki—his films are very self-reflexive, sometimes they may not have the stamp of his original filming. With Godard, you have to separate the films that were made outside the mainstream and his video work—most of his stuff. With his entire career, he wants to talk about all the things that you can possibly talk about in life, but he's going to do it by talking about film. He was a critic, and he changed: he needed to actualize his criticism by making films. In a certain sense, he still makes film criticism: he does it with the materials that he's criticizing. Who else am I forgetting here? Fassbinder, to a certain extent, I suppose.

JW: Like Fassbinder, you've gathered a repertory company of players for your films. . . .

HH: It's just a natural process when you work with someone and it goes well. Usually, when you make a film, you don't have enough time to learn anything except that you don't like a certain actor. If there is something interesting about the actor and they're doing good work, you're anxious to work with them again to reach a higher ground and do more ambitious work together. The problem is that casting is crucial. I always tell the people I'm working with, "Don't take this repertory stuff too seriously. Don't assume that you'll have a role in the next film!"

JW: Martin Donovan, your perennial lead, is missing from the cast of *Henry Fool*—could you have envisioned him in either of the lead roles?

HH: Henry was so inspired by Tom [Thomas Jay Ryan]. I had seen him on stage a number of times. I wanted someone unrecognizable. If I had used Martin, people would have said, "Oh, it's Martin Donovan, this is a Hal Hartley film." It would have been too clouded with expectations and associations, good and bad. Martin could certainly have done Henry. With my new film, he's playing Jesus. It's so obvious. As soon as I realized that I was writing this espionage movie about Jesus Christ in New York for the millennium, I thought, "This is a job for Martin Donovan!" He's such a lapsed Catholic, always brooding about it and so on.

JW: What do you feel is the greatest misconception or misrepresentation in terms of popular criticism of your work?

HH: Probably that it's not popular. They're certainly intended to be popular. Okay, it's not *Titanic*. There is a larger body for alternative films in most parts of the world outside America. Here, movies are kind of homogenized. I don't think that it's anything that the film industry does—people are just that way.

"Hal Hartley, Not So Simple"

Interview by Robert Avila, 2007. Originally appearing on SF360.org, the San Francisco Film Society's online magazine.

ROBERT AVILA: Do you see a lot of Hollywood movies? I was curious what you were reading and seeing these days.

HAL HARTLEY: In Berlin I go to a rental place. It's just amazing how people all over the world watch American movies, mainstream movies. So it gives me an opportunity to catch up on things—movies that I probably would not go to a movie theater to see. They're not that special to me, I don't have that much anticipation, but I do want to know what's going on.

RA: What have you seen lately?

HH: I saw, oh, they call it *High School Confidential* over there. It's the one about Evan Rachel Wood in high school. Oh god, what's it called here? It's a satire, real dark, these high school girls who fake a sexual harassment thing on a teacher. *Pretty Persuasion!* I thought that was pretty good. The writing was pretty good. And this girl, who was very young, who had been Rachel Wood [Kimberly Joyce], was really interesting. I actually see at least seven or eight films a week on DVD, and I do write them down, but my book is in Berlin. To tell you the truth, most of them go in and right out again. But the past couple years I've watched Terrence Malick's *Thin Red Line* at least once every two months. And *The New World,* which I just think is just extraordinary. I bought a DVD of that about a year ago. That's like a once-a-month thing.

RA: They're great films, poetic films, but what in particular draws you to them?

HH: It's of course the kind of filmmaking that I don't do at all, so it's not about that. But I learn from them. He's really great at telling the big old human-reality stories, in epic size. He gets great performances. He spends a lot of time looking at people's real characteristics and weaving them in. That's why they're very expensive films; they're certainly not sellout things. I think they're the best example of what big American filmmaking can be. And they're deep, and they're beautiful. His love of language and how he uses it is really quite great. I mean, that scene between Elias Koteas and Nick Nolte in *Thin Red Line,* when Koteas decides not to carry out the attacks the way Nolte wants him to, is just classic.

RA: I saw *Days of Heaven* again recently. They are like cinema's version of the novels.

HH: And he translates it into images, really good ones. A lot of the times, you think of a Malick film, you're not thinking about words. You're not thinking about dialogue, you're thinking about nature, you know there's this whole thing in every single one. You watch all four of those films, just the shots of the moon, the grass, human blood. Man in Nature. Man is natural, but Nature is against him. He's got a real serious thing he's working on. It's probably in his blood. And it's something I always forget, but how powerfully influenced I was right at the very beginning by *Days of Heaven* and *Badlands* in the seventies. I saw *Badlands* on TV late one night, in like 1975, 1976, and I was like [makes gesture of amazement]. I think probably my first group of Super-8 films through art school and into film school were very much like that—but without any understanding. [Laughter.]

RA: Were they narratives?

HH: They became narratives as I began to understand that there was such a thing as narrative. I had to have some older people, teachers, point that out.

RA: Are you conscious of how your approach to narrative has evolved over time?

HH: I think so. I mean, I keep notes about it. I not only write but I need to write about what I'm trying to do. So in reviewing my notes I can see. Part of it is changing interests. But part of it is also just having a more conscious understanding of what my instincts hold. It's only the past seven or eight years that I can really say I move people around in relation to the music of the dialogue. This is really clear now. I can watch films, *The Book of Life, No Such Thing;* I can see, yeah, this is telling an actor to walk across a room, pause, and say the line, go—the dialogue is really giving you the rhythm. It always doesn't work when you ignore it. Lots of interesting things can happen. I mean, Parker hears the rhythm of how I write perfectly well. I think it has to do with the amount of work she had to do being trained as an actress, to enunciate and to listen to poetry. Shakespeare, in her case, probably. So she has an ear for finding it. But there are other people who are really interesting who are different. Leo Fitzpatrick, in this film, is lovely to work with because he's got none of that. His entire rhythm of hearing as well as speaking, moving, couldn't be further away from how I hear it when I'm writing. But he's game. He says, "No, I want to do that." That gets really fun, too. Bill Sage is this way—you know, in *Girl from Monday, Simple Men*. He hears it. He can hear dialogue. But his rhythm—how people speak has to do with rhythms in their body, too. It was something early on in working with Bill in the early nineties that I was interested in this. He moved in this really weird way, like the pauses would come in really strange places, physically. In reaching for the drink he put in pauses and change-ups that didn't make any sense to me, basically. But as long as they know that there is rhythm here. You need to submit yourself to that rhythm. But that doesn't mean that everybody who does that sentence is going to do it the same way.

RA: The great actors one thinks of have of course very distinct ways of moving, different distinct rhythms.

HH: It's part of what attracts us to them, when we say, "Oh, I really love Humphrey Bogart," or something, it has to do with how he moves, how he thinks, and how he speaks.

RA: So it's a negotiation with the actor.

HH: Yeah, that's a good word. It would be dry and boring if it was just, "Here, you do it the way I want you to do it." I'm always watching them. There's kind of shorthand with some of these actors who I've worked a lot with, like Parker or Martin Donovan. Like, Parker will always say—I'll start telling people how it's going to happen. "Jeff, you're here at the table, Parker, you're here at the sink, then you're going to come over here." I'll talk for a little bit, and she'll say, "Just do it." And so I'll show her, and she watches. And then she does what I just did. And, of course, it's totally different. But then there's something I can watch. Then there's something I can look at. Once there's something I can look at, I can say, "Oh, that's great, but don't do that, take that part out." And I really stay on the outside of them. I can't presume to understand how they make these words and the situation real for them, so that it's a real, full performance. The inside I leave to them. But as long as everybody knows that the inside and the outside are connected, then there's a method of working. I deal with the outside. And it does change. This happens a lot, with Parker, this happens a lot: she'll be trying to do something, and it's not feeling right for her, and it's not right, therefore, for us, and I can introduce a pause. Now I'm listening to the dialogue really closely, and I'll often read the dialogue to myself, and I'll realize, yeah, she shouldn't be putting a pause in the middle of that sentence; she should just go. And I'll just watch the rehearsal that much more closely, and isolate the place, and say, "Don't put that pause in. Just run that whole line together." And you can see the understanding on the face when she does it. So that's a lot of what my work is when I'm on the set.

RA: Is there a lot of rehearsal time?

HH: No. Not like in the early days. Up through maybe *Amateur*, I used to put everyone on payroll for a month before we began shooting.

RA: That sounds unusual.

HH: Yeah, it was unusual. We'd work two, four days a week, maybe, as needed. But they were available, and we could work things out. And I think that was just because I always anticipated I wouldn't have time to discover things on set. And, in any event, I needed to understand more. And most of what I know about working with actors I really learned by working with actors. These things I say about the rhythm and the movement being tied directly to the rhythm of the dialogue—that's something that actors eventually pointed out to me. They at least put it in words, as I was still groping to understand what was happening.

RA: What was the experience working with Jeff Goldblum like?

HH: That was easy. Because he's one of those people who saw it right away. He didn't know my films that well; he was aware of them more. But he got the script, loved the script—but he also knew it was for Parker, and he wanted to work with Parker. But then he loved the script. Particularly, he said, "I love this kind of dialogue. I love this kind of thing." And then he started watching my movies, and he's the one who said, when we first met, he said, "You move people around." And I think he may have been the one who suggested that it's tied to the rhythm of the dialogue. He is really easy to work with. More than easy to work with, he's hilarious to work with. He's a complete child himself. [Laughter.] He's really considerate of everybody. He works to remember the names of the people who are on the truck unloading the equipment every morning, because he just wants everyone to like him and do their best to make him look good. So a really positive kind of energy. But so much energy, and so many ideas, that there's footage in the "making of" that comes on the DVD—I'm sure, it was unavoidable—but there's lots of me like listening to him, just nodding my head, letting him finish. But, great. We definitely want to work together again. It's really surprising, people have asked, "Why haven't you guys worked together before? He seems like the kind of Hal Hartley actor."

RA: I was going to say that. It's funny, I just saw *California Split* again. I think it's his first performance on screen.

HH: Yeah, he came up through that crowd.

RA: I was just struck by the beaming smile and enthusiasm with which we walks on.

HH: Alan Rudolph roped him into that gang. He's also in the election one.

RA: *Nashville*. Riding that enormous . . .

HH: Tricycle. [Laughter.]

RA: He doesn't really say anything in either film, but his presence is something else.

HH: Yeah, I think he said that Rudolph thought that he was interesting and then showed him to Altman and Altman said, "Yeah, we got to keep this guy around, I could use him somewhere."

RA: It sounds from what you just described that none of the enthusiasm you read there on the screen in those early films has dimmed.

HH: No, he loves his job. And everything that entails. And that means going around and being recognized as a celebrity, and the girls, and all this. He doesn't drink, he doesn't smoke, he gets up at four o'clock in the morning and reads scripts, goes to the gym and works out, goes for a run. You meet him at seven o'clock in the morning and he's done all this, and he's bright as a bulb. "What do we do now? Can we go to work now?" [Laughter.] He's sort of like that.

RA: Is it films that mainly structure your life? Working for the next film?

HH: Less so now. Yeah, it's less so.

RA: What structures your life between films?

HH: Business. Between two full days to four full days a week, I have to take care of things. But I've been working for like three years now to make that change. I just licensed a bunch of early films to a sales agent who's going to be taking care of all that stuff now. So, theoretically, I could be down to just one day a week.

RA: Is that daunting? What would you do with the other six days?

HH: Write! I should be getting up in the morning and just writing.

RA: Are there periods when writing is difficult, even when business isn't in the way?

HH: I've felt sometimes I've had to stop, to walk away from something. But usually I have different projects. If I'm feeling one needs to be digested a little bit more or thought about, I can go to another. But sometimes you just shouldn't write. Some novelists have told me, I think Paul Auster told me, sometimes you just can't, you just got to go out, do something else for a week. I've never had trouble writing. But it's an interesting question about structure. In the early nineties, my life was totally about making films. I felt if I was finishing one and I didn't have one lined up already, I was shirking or something. I guess at the beginning of my career I just couldn't believe I was getting away with this. Somebody's going to find out, and it will end. [Laughter.] So I was just working all the time. But by the time I got married, I remember, in 1996, and I decided—I had been trying to work in different ways, too. I mean, making feature films is great, and I think I'm good at it, and I've learned a lot. The whole world comes to me through that work. But often I'd like to do something more than supply anticipated product for a known market, which is what it always becomes. No matter how much you try to push the envelope, it's got to be a certain length [and so on]. And I think I made a big effort to do that from the end of *Henry Fool* on. When I finished *Henry Fool,* I thought that was it, I don't know if I'll make another feature for a long time. And I started more of the experimental work. I got a studio on Fourteenth Street in New York and set up kind of a workshop. And all those short films come out of there, and *The Book of Life.* Actually, *The Book of Life, No Such Thing,* and *The Girl from Monday* really all come out from that time. If *No Such Thing* had been made on digital video like the other two, I think it would be more obviously a trilogy.

RA: Do you anticipate making more short films?

HH: Yeah, I've made a couple. They come, oddly. I made something when Miho and I went to Japan to attend her sister's wedding. We stayed there for a while; we stayed in Japan for like a month. And I made something out of that, which is about being middle-aged and married, and culture. I just went really to make a video of her family to show my family, because I'm sure they're never going to meet each other. I mean, her family are farmers, in the mountains, and getting to Tokyo about twice in a lifetime is a big deal.

RA: So that's where you were staying?

HH: Yeah. It's not too remote, but it's rural and they're farmers, so you can't get away from the land. And my father is eighty-three now, so he's not going to go to Japan. So I was making footage of that, but it kind of turned into a meditation on our life at this point.

RA: Is that a private film, or is it something you'll eventually distribute?

HH: I will distribute it eventually. I think when I accumulate enough smaller things that speak to each other in a good way then I'll put it together.

RA: It sounds liberating to make a short film like that on your own on the spur of the moment. Or did you have help?

HH: No, that was it. It was just me. I had this bag and my VX100, a microphone. And Miho and I interviewed each other.

RA: It reminds me of Godard and Miéville.

HH: Or *Soft and Hard.* I thought about *Soft and Hard,* where he and Anne-Marie talk to each other about things.

RA: About life together.

HH: Yeah, they're talking about a lot of things. They're two smart people, it's hard to kind of keep up. [Laughter.]

RA: Was that the first time you'd done something like that together?

HH: Yes. On the plane to Japan, I told her, I said, "Why don't you think about ten questions you want to ask me, and I'll get ten questions I want to ask you."

RA: And were the questions asked to you on camera for the first time?

HH: I just made a shot of her, and she had the microphone on, and I just let it run, and I talked to her. I mean, we didn't use it all, but it's a useful thing to structure the other footage we made.

RA: Did it make you particularly nervous?

HH: Yeah, me, definitely. Being on camera is enough to make me nervous, but also talking about serious subjects, of course I'm nervous. But that's what you do. [Laughter.] You kind of force yourself into a scary place.

RA: This is the third film you've made outside the United States. What opportunities does filming abroad afford you?

HH: Earlier, they'd been aesthetic reasons [for shooting abroad]; there was nothing economic about it. This one posed certain problems. I was already living in Berlin, and the script, of course, had been written for Queens, but also for Paris and Istanbul. It's not a totally small film, but we didn't have the money to travel to all these places and do all these things there. And we couldn't base it out of New York, either. It's just become too expensive there. So then we just reread the script. One thing I discovered right off the bat is that like 90 percent of the movie is indoors, which is unusual. So we started thinking about sets, building sets that would match the first film. But we got lucky. It was mostly about Parker's, Fay's, home. At the eleventh hour we found a German prefab Bauhaus neighborhood that had these homes that could be Queens, or Brooklyn. We had to change a lot of the details, but the layout could definitely be a home in Brooklyn. It was just a lot of work doing location scouting, finding the interior of the French Ministry. Those kinds of things were easier because European cities all have that monumental eighteenth-century [building] somewhere.

RA: Did this slow you down at all?

HH: No, we shot as fast as I've usually had to shoot in the United States. It's only twenty-eight days, I think—less, like twenty-six. No, certain things were harder to find, like the big set for Fay's home. That took us a long time. This really good locations guy, Roland Gerhardt, at the eleventh hour found [it]. Because a lot of the page count—if it's a 130-page script, seventy pages happen in Fay's house. So we knew that if we shot for twenty-six days we were at that location for like six or seven. Other things were kind of easy.

RA: You say you were living in Berlin at the time. I read you were a fellow at the American Academy of Berlin. What were you doing there exactly?

HH: Well, it's a kind of colony, like the MacDowell Colony, so they give you a stipend for three months to work on something that ostensibly has something to do with American-German relations or history, or just about Germany. I'd been working on a script for a long time about the life of Simone Weil, the French social activist, and she had spent some time in Berlin before the war. That seemed to be enough.

RA: Are you still working on that project?

HH: Yeah, but it's a long way off.

RA: She's a fascinating figure. A deep thinker, but also a pacifist willing to join the French resistance and so on.

HH: She's a much more representative person of the time and the place than people think.

RA: So you were based there.

HH: And I liked it. My wife, Miho, and I decided that some changes needed to be made. It was getting difficult to be in New York. A lot of our friends had left after the Patriot Act and things came in. We just really didn't feel like that was the center of our lives anymore.

RA: So that's where you're based now?

HH: Berlin is where we're based. We keep a small apartment in New York, because she's designing fashion and that work is in New York.

RA: Getting out of the United States, I think it's probably a widespread urge these days.

HH: It's uncomfortable here. It's subtle. You don't realize; the devil is in the details. You only realize after a couple of years, these laws that seem so abstract when you read about them in the paper, how they really are affecting your life.

RA: Do you feel very far away in Berlin?

HH: No, I feel really at home in Berlin. Even though I can't speak the language, if you can believe it. Much more at home than I've ever felt in the United States outside New York. And I guess New York was simply because of the density of family and friends.

RA: I've found, living outside the country, it can be nice not to speak the language.

HH: In a way it's very calming. I feel really calm walking around Berlin. It's sort of an existential disconnect. Sometimes I used to hyperventilate, when I was first there. What happens if I get hurt? And I need to go to the hospital or I need help from my neighbors? Now I've accumulated a little bit more German. But there is that peace. When I leave my home, workshop, and I go down onto the street, I really feel free. I don't have any obligations. It's really quite nice to be an expat. Also, the normal expectations of what one needs for one's regular day is so different than in America. You see it with kids most obviously, with families. The poorest American I know who has a child has to have a separate room for all the child's toys. Whereas in Germany and France it's just not that way. We have such a weird insistence on giving them all that. They actually deal with the kids in a way. [Laughter.]

RA: I'm wondering if being an artist in an environment where you don't necessarily speak the language can help you focus.

HH: It lends a focus, that's true. I guess certain people in my position might take a house in Spain, by the ocean, to really get away from everybody and work on something. Well, I'm a city person. I can't go too far into the country. I don't like to drive or anything. So Berlin is that place for me. I'm in the midst of the city. But one of the things I love about Berlin is that it's got all the great things of a city, but also it feels like being in the country, really. There are so many trees; they have a big insistence on a kind of calmness, you know, the weekends are the weekends. I can be in my flat in Berlin for weeks at a time and not see anybody if I don't want to. So I have been getting a lot done, preparing more work.

RA: Do you find opportunities for creative mistranslation?

HH: A lot of my writing, of course, now has to do with this, an American being in Germany, or Europe generally, and miscommunications and discoveries that you only make in that manner.

RA: Did you see Fay operating that way?

HH: No, I can't say that those kinds of things affected that because Fay was written before. That was written in the years I was working at Harvard [2001 to 2004].

RA: Did you always know you wanted to continue the story of Henry Fool?

HH: Using the word "continue" is funny. It might be more accurate to say that I knew for a long time that I would like to make up a new story that utilized these same people. It's the disjunction from one movie to another that will come to typify these films, I think.

RA: Have people been commenting on how different they are as films?

HH: Most people just, rightly so, fixate on the characters. They ask, "How was it to think what Fay would be like ten years later? How would she have grown from that girl?" But in fact there's lots of evidence in the first film. That's where I went when I tried to figure out what I was going to make up to tell a new story with these people: I went back to the first film and made notes. Henry mentions South America; Henry mentions Paris. But for Fay's character, towards the end, you could see that she's not the same girl she was at the beginning. When she takes her son out of the topless bar where he's drinking with his father—she's already gotten a little bit more responsible. And when she looks at the neighbor's girl, Pearl, coming out of the house, which has to do with some bad shit going on with the stepfather. She started almost clueless, but she's learning.

RA: Initially she's just young, irresponsible, demanding. . . .

HH: She just wants to get fucked. [Laughs.]

RA: It must have been tempting to continue her development.

HH: It was. We just looked at what would be the most likely changes that would happen in a person, if they were raising a kid by themselves. And certain kinds of sadnesses have happened—her mother committing suicide in the bathroom, her husband going off somewhere because he killed the next-door neighbor, and her brother in prison. So there's sadness and difficulty there that she's got to bear up under. For the purposes of this movie, I really wanted her to be the representative American of a particular type that I hope exists somewhere out there. She's perfectly well-intentioned, but she's uninformed, which I think you can say about a lot of the population here. But then, she's actually quite smart and quite brave and deeply charitable. That's the tragedy in this film. If she didn't waste time trying to make sure that Bebe came along with them, she would have been reunited with Henry. So we'll have to deal with that in part three.

RA: It's interesting, too, how Henry does and doesn't develop. In terms of their relationship, specifically, he was always moving away from her in the first film.

HH: He didn't want to be married. He was afraid of being tied down. But he was terribly drawn to her sexually.

RA: It finally gets him to the altar.

HH: Yeah, he's just a slob. [Laughs.] He's just a child. But I believe him at the end of *Henry Fool*. He says, "I love you, Fay." And she kisses him and says, "Tough." [Laughs.] I'm just curious, in my writing now for what will eventually become part three, I guess, I really want to understand more now about the nature of the attraction between them. I don't really see this movie as being about this great romantic love, and she'll do anything to be with the man she loves. I think she's over that. She's trying to bring the family together.

RA: It struck me that he's still as restless and rambunctious as ever, but now it's writ large in terms of geopolitics and international intrigue.

HH: The first one's about the individual, Simon really, and the nature of influence. But to really simplify it: the first one's about the creative act; the effect on the individual, the family, the community, culture. And then the second one is starting with the culture, but you're seeing it through the prism of the experience of a certain family, a certain woman. So the third one, I think, will be different again. I'm feeling the rhythm of a conclusion happening. The third one will almost, I think, speak to the first one as much as the second.

RA: How was it working with the same actors ten years later? Liam Aiken, as the now teenaged Ned, for instance?

HH: That was his first role, when he was six years old. It's his very first time in the movies. And he's a good kid. He's smart, and he's into it. I asked him already, I said, "Look, this is definitely moving towards a number three, and that will definitely be about Ned." He's a guitarist, too, he's got a band. So I asked him, "Are you gonna stay an actor? Can I count on you for a third one?" And he said yeah. But it's funny about Henry. Tom Ryan and I had this conversation about how he would be different. I remember Tom articulating it really well, saying, "No, Henry doesn't change. Henry is exactly the slob, the childish, self-involved but hilarious guy that he's always been. The context changes but he's like a rock at the center." I think there's something in that. I think the third one could be really quite hard on him, without bashing him, but coming to the brutal truth about a character like that. I could definitely see the son saying, "You know, Mom's in a Turkish prison." Or, think about it, if Fay is accused of treason by the United States—we're the only country in the world that kills people for this. She could be executed. You can be executed. It could really come down hard on his father. This could definitely be a Luke Skywalker/Darth Vader type thing, like he's going to kill the old man. But I could imagine him finally not doing it because he understands that this man is just a child. He's a perpetual child. He doesn't know what the implications are of everything that happens to him.

RA: There's also something mythical about him.

HH: Even before I wanted to make the second one, I wanted to make a contemporary American classic of the Faust type. And he was the Mephistopheles, and Simon is the Faust. Even when Goethe and Marlowe were doing their Fausts, Faust was already a stock, standard story. I think something about the perennial [nature] of these characters means that I can work with them for a long, long time. We'll have to see.

RA: You've always scored your films yourself, and the music is invariably an integral element in them. How do you go about creating the music?

HH: Usually, it's the old fashioned way. I cut the picture and the dialogue, and then they're on cassette tapes—although I should be doing this on computer now. Anyway, so I have a TV, and I'll just play to it. Maybe while I've been making the film and editing it I'll tinker around with piano trying to find themes. In this case, it was quite fun, because this *Henry Fool* music already existed. So I listened a lot to the music I made in 1996 and 1997. It took me a long time to find that chord [hums main theme], which is a classic, carnival, gypsy-type thing. But I couldn't remember the actual [chord]. I finally found it. I wrote it down. I think only once do you actually hear the chords played that way—I think it's on the CD, but it's not in the movie—but the rhythm is played as an arpeggio. That kind of opened up a whole world. I think the music here is very much more affected by music from *No Such Thing* and *The Girl from Monday*. It's less machine music than *The Girl from Monday*. But *The Girl from Monday* also, the kind of strategy there was mechanical music with acoustic instruments. There are lots of cellos and clarinets—but also program drumming, banging, electric guitars, and stuff. This one left that kind of stuff out, but it's mostly an instrumentation that's been evolving since *No Such Thing*.

RA: Do you play with other musicians?

HH: In that sense, it's all mechanical, it's all done [by me] on keyboard.

RA: Did you study music?

HH: No. I studied classical guitar when I was a teenager, and some sight-reading then. Actually, in the year before *Henry Fool,* my music partner for a long time, Jeff Taylor, moved back here to the West Coast to start another career. When we made all that music from *Simple Men, Amateur, Flirt,* I was always at the instruments, and he was doing the thinking about harmony and theory, and would suggest things. I really grew dependent on him. When he was leaving, I said, "Okay, we're going to have to get serious about this." So I took a thirteen-week night course at the New School on sight-reading, which just reminded me of all that stuff I knew as a kid. And it gave me a lot of confidence. Without a doubt, *Henry Fool* was the most confident music I had made myself. Jeff thought so, too. He called me immediately when he saw the film and said, "Very good work." So since then I've had a lot more confidence.

RA: Do you enjoy playing music generally? Is it a daily activity?

HH: No, it's really dictated by movies. I almost never—this is a typical circumstance: in eight weeks, nine weeks while we're doing the sound editing on *Fay Grim* in one room, I'm in another room, where I spend most of the day making music and recording it. When I feel I have a bunch for one part of the movie, I'll go over into the next room, and I'll put it into the computer. That's all pretty exciting. I generate an enormous amount of music that way. Then we do the mix of the film, and I'm away from the music for another month. Then, when everything chills out, and the movie's done, and it's delivered, and my time is my own again, I usually go back and start listening to all the recordings again, thinking to put together a CD. So I'm looking for the best and the most representative. And that leads to me redoing them—because music in movies needs to be less than it is if you're just listening to it in a room. Trying to redo it as a listening experience solely, that's great. I love that. That's the only time I'm just being a musician every day. Then I'm finished, and I probably won't take the sheet off the keyboard until the next time.

RA: Do you follow music in Berlin?

HH: I see a lot of classical, jazz, and contemporary orchestral stuff. I like to go to bed too early to keep up with the rock scene. I have lots of rocker friends who I just can't—I never see them rock.

RA: Your reapproach to the filmmaking process, technically and aesthetically, in *The Girl from Monday,* with the digital cameras, smaller crews, et cetera: how did it feed the production of *Fay Grim?*

HH: It's the smaller movies, the things that I've been shooting in conventional DV cam, that led me to start doing all the Dutch angles, for instance, playing around with that kind of stylistic [approach]. But also those three films that preceded it were all conceived around the same time. It was part of a larger project (I'm talking about *The Book of Life, No Such Thing,* and *The Girl from Monday*) to treat a certain big subject—faith and the body, or our spiritual life and the body—from different angles, all using genres. So I did a lot of studying of genres. With *No Such Thing,* watching monster movies of every variety. Asking, What do all of these movies have in common? There are always funny things. In so many of the Japanese *Mothra* movies, and *Godzilla,* it's a female journalist who has to go out and investigate—those common things I wanted to draw on. I think I was quite studied in that kind of research. So when I knew that *Fay Grim* would have to start as a kind of espionage-thriller satire, I knew exactly what to do. Get the newspapers, get real things out of the international section; and reading spy novels, watching spy movies.

RA: So you immersed yourself in those kinds of sources?

HH: And became sharper at saying, "This is something that happens in every spy movie, whether it's *James Bond* or it's *The Spy Who Came In from the Cold,* there's always that moment when there's a flip, when the person she trusts turns out to be lying, not who he was." It's good. Sometimes making use of a genre can allow you to treat quite serious stuff in a light manner. You can be in fact more poetic about it—in a way, a little bit more ridiculous about it—and still maintain a little sincerity.

RA: So it frees you.

HH: It can, yeah. Giving yourself to a form, or to a genre, as we say it in storytelling. You hear musicians talking about this. They say, I have all these ideas, but I don't know if it should be a fugue or some other form. They feel it, they hear it, but they haven't discovered yet what's the best form for it.

RA: Prior to this, you hadn't concerned yourself consciously with genre?

HH: Only with *Amateur.* And that was very early on. I didn't do quite as much of that research. Back then I didn't try to look for those typical things. I just remembered detective shows from television in the seventies and was kind of working off of what I remembered.

RA: I was looking over that interview you conducted with Godard back in 1994. There was a question you asked him about new technologies, the possibilities concerning new modes and networks of distribution and so on. He was a little dismissive or pessimistic about it, but you seemed enthusiastic.

HH: That's what everyone was talking about in my group. He talks poetically, so it's hard to sort it out, but I don't think he's quite as pessimistic as it sounds brutally right there on the page. In a way, he's just admitting that times are changing. But it's like the political economy of filmmaking, he sees ridiculous things, like it's clearly moving toward smaller screens. Doesn't he say something like that?

RA: He does.

HH: "The apartments are getting smaller, so why should the screens get bigger?" I think he's nostalgic for the old, big, communal experience. But I'm certain that at that time that was not how he experienced films anymore. It's not like he went out to the movie theater. He had, like, Tom Luddy sending him DVDs of everything.

RA: Although he wasn't far off, seeing as everybody watches movies on their computers, and my apartment, anyway, keeps shrinking.

HH: He wasn't, no.

RA: More than ten years later, what do you see, with the realization of these new networks? The San Francisco Film Festival, for example, has a pilot project this year to send films out over the Internet rather than bringing films and people exclusively into the physical festival grounds per the old paradigm. Do you see yourself in these new distribution networks?

HH: Yeah, of course. I think at that time, in 1994, I probably believed these things would be a choice for us. And now I understand, this is not a choice. Movies are a commercial art, and commerce will determine how people enjoy them. It's always been that way, from nickelodeons on. So I don't sweat it anymore. A film like *Fay Grim*, it's made with new technology, but it in fact is doing what movies were doing seventy, eighty years ago. But, yeah, the manner of getting it out to people is different. And there are people who know more about that than I do. I'm not really going to sweat it so much.

RA: You're still doing basically what you've always done?

HH: In some ways. When I was here [in San Francisco] with *The Girl from Monday*, that was probably the most radical thing I've ever done, to think, "Well, we've made this movie in such a different, alternative manner, what would happen if we just amplified that a little bit more and just considered distribution as part of the production process?" You know, I don't regret doing it, but it was way, way too much work.

RA: To do it yourself?

HH: Yeah, to take it around the country . . . but that would be considered terribly old-fashioned now.

Feature-length Films

The Unbelievable Truth (1989)
United States
Production: Action Features
Producers: Jerome Brownstein, Hal Hartley, Bruce Weiss
Distribution: Overseas Film Group, First Look Media
Director: Hal Hartley
Screenplay: Hal Hartley
Cinematography: Michael Spiller
Editors: Nick Gomez, Hal Hartley
Sound: Nick Gomez, Jeff Kushner
Music: Jim Coleman, Hal Hartley, Kendall Brothers, Phil Reed, Wild Blue
    Yonder
Production Designer: Carla Gerona
Costume Designer: Kelly Reichardt
Cast: Adrienne Shelly (Audry Hugo), Robert John Burke (Josh Hutton),
    Christopher Cooke (Vic Hugo), Julia McNeal (Pearl), Katherine Mayfield
    (Liz Hugo), Gary Sauer (Emmet), Mark Bailey (Mike), David Healy (Todd
    Whitbred), Matt Malloy (Otis), Edie Falco (Jane), Paul Schulze (Bill),
    Mike Brady (Bob), Bill Sage (Gus)
Color
90 min.
35mm

Trust (1990)
United States, United Kingdom
Production: True Fiction Pictures in association with Film Four
    International, Zenith Productions Ltd.
Producers: Jerome Brownstein, Ted Hope, Scott Meek, Bruce Weiss
Distribution: Fortissimo Films
Director: Hal Hartley

Screenplay: Hal Hartley
Cinematography: Michael Spiller
Editor: Nick Gomez
Sound: Tom Paul, Jeff Pullman, Kate Sanford, Reilly Steele
Music: Philip Reed, "Walk Away," "Mess with Me" (Hub Moore and the
     Great Outdoors); "Symphony No. 5 in C Minor" (Beethoven; unnamed
     performance)
Production Designer: Dan Ouellette
Costume Designer: Claudia Brown
Cast: Adrienne Shelly (Maria Coughlin), Martin Donovan (Matthew
     Slaughter), Rebecca Merritt Nelson (Jean Coughlin), John MacKay (Jim
     Slaughter), Gary Sauer (Anthony), Matt Malloy (Ed), Susanne Costollos
     (Rachel), Jeffrey Howard (Robert), Karen Sillas (Nurse Paine), Tom
     Thon (Deli Man), M. C. Bailey (Bruce), Patricia Sullivan (Ruark Boss),
     Marko Hunt (John Coughlin), Bill Sage (John Bill), Julie Sukman (Biker
     Mom)
Color
107 min.
35mm

Surviving Desire (1991)
United States
Production: American Playhouse, True Fiction Pictures
Producers: Jerome Brownstein, Ted Hope
Distribution: Possible Films
Director: Hal Hartley
Screenplay: Hal Hartley
Cinematography: Michael Spiller
Editors: Steve Hamilton, Hal Hartley
Sound: Jeff Pullman, Reilly Steele
Music: Hal Hartley (as Ned Rifle), The Great Outdoors, "Drug Test" (Yo La
     Tengo)
Production Designer: Steven Rosenzweig
Cast: Martin Donovan (Jude), Mary B. Ward (Sofie), Matt Malloy (Henry),
     Rebecca Merritt Nelson (Katie), Julie Sukman (Jill), Hub Moore, John
     Sharples, Dan Castelli, and Craig Adams (The Great Outdoors)
Color
60 min.
16mm

Simple Men (1992)
United States, United Kingdom, Italy
Production: American Playhouse Theatrical Films in association with Fine

Line Features, BIM Distribuzione, True Fiction Pictures in association with Film Four International, Zenith Productions Ltd.
Producers: Jerome Brownstein, Hal Hartley, Ted Hope, Bruce Weiss
Distribution: Capitol Films
Director: Hal Hartley
Screenplay: Hal Hartley
Cinematography: Michael Spiller
Editor: Steve Hamilton
Sound: Jeff Pullman, Reilly Steele
Music: Hal Hartley (as Ned Rifle), "Kool Thing" (Sonic Youth); "Always Something," "Some Kinda Fatigue," "Sleeping Pill" (Yo La Tengo)
Production Designer: Daniel Ouellette
Costume Designer: Alexandra Welker
Cast: Robert John Burke (Bill McCabe), Bill Sage (Dennis McCabe), Karen Sillas (Kate), Elina Löwensohn (Elina), Martin Donovan (Martin), Mark Chandler Bailey (Mike), Christopher Cooke (Vic), Jeffrey Howard (Ned Rifle), Holly Marie Combs (Kim), Joe Stevens (Jack), Damian Young (Sheriff), Marietta Marich (Mrs. McCabe), John MacKay (William McCabe), Bethany Wright (Mary), Richard Reyes (Security Guard), James Hansen Prince (Frank), Vivian Lanko (Nun), Mary McKenzie (Vera), Matt Malloy (Boyish Cop)
Color
105 min.
35mm

Amateur (1993)
United States, United Kingdom, France
Production: Channel Four Films, La Sept Cinéma, True Fiction Pictures, UGC in association with American Playhouse Theatrical Films, Zenith Productions Ltd.
Producers: Jerome Brownstein, Hal Hartley, Ted Hope, Lindsay Law, Yves Marmion, Scott Meek
Distribution: UGC Images
Director: Hal Hartley
Screenplay: Hal Hartley
Cinematography: Michael Spiller
Editor: Steve Hamilton
Sound: Marko A. Costanzo, Jeanne Gilliland, Paul Koronkiewicz, Susan Littenberg, Jeff Pullman, Steve Silkensen, Reilly Steele
Music: Hal Hartley (as Ned Rifle), Jeffrey Taylor, "Mind Full of Worry" (Aquanetta); "Only Shallow" (My Bloody Valentine); "Water" (P. J. Harvey); "Japanese to English" (Red House Painters); "Shaker" (Yo La Tengo);

"Tom Boy" (Bettie Serveert); "Girls! Girls! Girls!" (Liz Phair); "Then
Comes Dudley" (The Jesus Lizard); "Here" (Pavement)
Production Designer: Steven Rosenzweig
Costume Designer: Alexandra Welker
Cast: Isabelle Huppert (Isabelle), Martin Donovan (Thomas Ludens), Elina
Löwensohn (Sofia Ludens), Damian Young (Edward), Chuck Montgomery
(Jan), Dave Simonds (Kurt), Pamela Stewart (Officer Patsy Melville), Erica
Gimpel (Irate Woman), Jan Leslie Harding (Waitress), Michael Imperioli
(Doorman at Club), David Greenspan (George, the Pornographer),
Adria Tennor (Kid Reading *The Odyssey*), Parker Posey (Girl Squatter),
Dwight Ewell (Boy Squatter), Patricia Scanlon (Young Irate Mother), Dael
Oriandersmith (Mother Superior), Michael Gaston (Sharpshooter), Paul
Schulze (Cop Who Shoots Thomas)
Color
105 min.
35mm

Flirt (1995)
United States, Germany, Japan
Production: Possible Films
Producers: Jerome Brownstein, Reinhard Brundig, Martin Hagerman, Ted
Hope, Satoru Iseki
Distribution: Fortissimo Films
Director: Hal Hartley
Screenplay: Hal Hartley
Cinematography: Michael Spiller
Editors: Steve Hamilton, Hal Hartley
Sound: Pietro Cecchini, Jeanne Gilliland, Jeff Pullman, Jennifer Ralston,
Steve Silkensen
Music: Hal Hartley (as Ned Rifle), Jeffrey Taylor, "Paris Is Waiting" (Lost,
Lonely, and Vicious); "House Sleeps Fire" (She Never Blinks); "Tavasz
Tavasz" (Marta Sebesten); "Alley Way" (J. F. Colemen Jr.); "Every Waking
Hour" (Lou Mulkern); "Crushed Impalas" (The Miss Alans)
Production Designer: Steven Rosenzweig
Costume Designer: Alexandra Welker
Cast: *New York, February 1993:* Parker Posey (Emily), Bill Sage (Bill),
Martin Donovan (Walter), Paul Austin (Man No. 3), Robert John Burke
(Man No. 2), Erica Gimpel (Nurse), Michael Imperioli (Michael), Karen
Sillas (Doctor Clint), Hannah Sullivan (Trish)
Berlin, October 1994: Dominik Bender (Johann), Dwight Ewell (Dwight),
Geno Lechner (Greta), Elina Löwensohn (Nurse), Peter Fitz (The
Doctor), Maria Schrader (Girl in Phone Booth)

Tokyo, March 1995: Miho Nikaido (Miho), Toshizo Fujiwara (Ozu), Chikako Hara (Yuki), Kumiko Ishizuka (Naomi), Hal Hartley (Hal, uncredited)
Color
85 min.
35mm

Henry Fool (1997)
United States
Production: True Fiction Pictures
Producers: Keith Abell, Jerome Brownstein, Thierry Cagianut, Hal Hartley, Larry Meistrich, Daniel J. Victor
Distribution: Fortissimo Films
Director: Hal Hartley
Screenplay: Hal Hartley
Cinematography: Michael Spiller
Editor: Steve Hamilton
Sound: Daniel McIntosh, David Paterson, David Raphael, Reilly Steele, Karl Wasserman
Music: Hal Hartley, Jim Coleman; Ryful (Jim Coleman, Bill Dobrow, Hal Hartley, Lydia Kavanagh, and Hub Moore)
Production Designer: Steven Rosenzweig
Costume Designer: Jocelyn Josen
Cast: Thomas Jay Ryan (Henry Fool), James Urbaniak (Simon Grim), Parker Posey (Fay Grim), Maria Porter (Mary Grim), Kevin Corrigan (Warren), James Saito (Mr. Deng), Miho Nikaido (Gnoc Deng), Jan Leslie Harding (Vicky), Diana Ruppe (Amy), Veanne Cox (Laura), Nicholas Hope (Father Hawkes), Gene Ruffini (Officer Buñuel), Liam Aiken (Ned), Chaylee Worrall (Pearl Age 7), Christy Carlson Romano (Pearl Age 14), Chuck Montgomery (Angus James), Don Creech (Owen Feer), Camille Paglia (Herself), Dave Simonds (Bill)
Color
137 min.
35mm

The Book of Life (1998)
United States, France
Production: La Sept Arte, Haut et Court, True Fiction Pictures
Producers: Simon Arnal, Caroline Benjo, Jerome Brownstein, Thierry Cagianut, Pierre Chevalier, Chelsea Fuhrer, Matthew Myers, Carole Scotta
Distribution: Celluloid Dreams
Director: Hal Hartley
Screenplay: Hal Hartley

Cinematography: Jim Denault
Editor: Steve Hamilton
Sound: David Paterson, Jeff Pullman, Reilly Steele
Music: "Polorum Regina" (Osnabruker Jugend Chor); "The Faster I Breathe the Further I Go" (P. J. Harvey); "In a Hole" (Phylr); "1.666666" (Takako Minekawa); "Two People" (Hub); "Turtle Soup" (Yo La Tengo); "Waking Up" (Miss Crabtree); "My Name Is Rich" (Joey Sweeney); "Machu Picchu" (David Byrne); "Mrs. Nedelija Became Famous" (Le Mystere Des Voix Bulgares); "King of Boys" (Lydia Kavanagh); "Lincoln" (Super 5 Thor); "Far from the Sun" (Drazy Hoops); "Love Too Soon" (Pascal Comelade and P. J. Harvey); "Fugitive" (Ryful); "Laudamus Virginem" (Osnabruker Jugend Chor)
Art Director: Andy Biscontini
Costume Designer: Monica Willis
Cast: Martin Donovan (Jesus Christ), P. J. Harvey (Magdalena), Thomas Jay Ryan (Satan), Miho Nikaido (Edie), Martin Pfefferkorn (Martyr), Paul Albe (Mormon Thug No. 1), Don Creech (Mormon Thug No. 2), William S. Burroughs (Preacher Voice on Radio), Katreen Hardt (Lawyer's Assistant), Georgia Hubley, Ira Kaplan, and James McNew (Salvation Army Band), D. J. Mendel (Lawyer), Dave Simonds (Dave), James Urbaniak (True Believer)
Color
63 min.
Digital Video

No Such Thing (2001)
United States, Iceland
Production: United Artists Films, American Zoetrope Production, the Icelandic Film Corporation, True Fiction Pictures, Monster Productions
Producers: Willi Baer, Francis Ford Coppola, Fridrik Thor Fridriksson, Hal Hartley, Linda Reisman, Cecelia Kate Roque
Distribution: Hollywood Classics Ltd.
Director: Hal Hartley
Screenplay: Hal Hartley
Cinematography: Michael Spiller
Editor: Steve Hamilton
Sound: Kjartan Kjartansson, Andrew Kris, George Lara, Jennifer Ralston, Reilly Steele
Music: Hal Hartley
Production Designer: Arni Pall Johannsson
Costume Designer: Helga I. Stefansdottir
Make-Up Effects: Mark Rappaport, the Creature Effects Company
Cast: Robert John Burke (the Monster), Sarah Polley (Beatrice), Julie

Christie (Dr. Anna), Baltasar Kormákur (Artaud), D.J. Mendel (Agent), Helen Mirren (The Boss), Miho Nikaido (Beautician), Bill Sage (Carlo), James Urbaniak (Concierge), Damian Young (Berger)
Color
102 min.
35mm

The Girl from Monday (2005)
United States
Production: Possible Films, Mad Mad Judy, Monday Company
Producers: Steve Hamilton, Hal Hartley, Lisa Porter
Distribution: Fortissimo Films
Director: Hal Hartley
Screenplay: Hal Hartley
Cinematography: Sarah Cawley Cabiya
Editor: Steve Hamilton
Sound: Dan Brashi, Justin Kawashima, Andrew Kris, Jeff Pullman
Music: Hal Hartley
Production Designers: Nick Carbonaro, Richard Sylvarnes, Inbal Weinberg
Costume Designers: Virginia Cook, Miho Nikaido
Choreography: David Neumann
Cast: Bill Sage (Jack), Sabrina Lloyd (Cecile), Tatiana Abracos (the Girl from Monday), Leo Fitzpatrick (William), D. J. Mendel (Abercrombie), James Urbaniak (Funk), Juliana Francis (Rita), Michael Cassidy (Ted), Normandy Sherwood (Emily), James Stanley (Doc), Paul Urbanski (CEO), Edie Falco (Judge), Matt Kalman (Nick), Tanya Perez (Theresa), Jenny Seastone Stern (Martha), Linda Horwatt (Rachel)
Color
84 min.
Digital Video

Fay Grim (2006)
United States, Germany
Production: HDNet Films, Possible Films, This Is That Productions, Zero Film GmbH
Producers: Julien Berlan, Mark Cuban, Martin Hagemann, Hal Hartley, Ted Hope, Mike King, Jason Kliot, Mike S. Ryan, Joana Vicente, Todd Wagner, Maren Wölk, Özlem Yurtsever
Distribution: HDNet International
Director: Hal Hartley
Screenplay: Hal Hartley
Cinematography: Sarah Cawley
Editor: Hal Hartley

Sound: David Jung, Christian Lutz, Paul Oberle, Matthias Schwab
Music: Hal Hartley
Production Designer: Richard Sylvarnes
Costume Designer: Anette Guther
Cast: Parker Posey (Fay Grim), D. J. Mendel (Father Lang), Liam
  Aiken (Ned), Megan Gay (Principal), Jasmin Tabatabai (Milla), Chuck
  Montgomery (Angus James), James Urbaniak (Simon Grim), Jeff
  Goldblum (Agent Fulbright), Leo Fitzpatrick (Carl Fogg), J. E. Heys
  (Herzog), Harald Schrott (Andre), Miho Nikaido (Gnoc Deng), Elina
  Löwensohn (Bebe), Peter Benedict (Raul Picard), Tim Seyfi (Rabbi
  Todorov), Hubert Mulzer (Minister of Security), Mehdi Nebbou (Islamic
  Cleric), Saffron Burrows (Juliet), Nikolai Kinski (Amin), Thomas Jay Ryan
  (Henry Fool), Jef Bayonne (French Drug Dealer), Sibel Kekilli (Concierge
  First Istanbul Hotel), Erdal Yildiz (Concierge Second Istanbul Hotel),
  Anatole Taubman (Jallal)
Color
118 min.
HDCAM Digital Video

Short Films

For short films prior to 1991 and music videos, see Hartley and Kaleta,
True Fiction Pictures and Possible Films.

Ambition (1991)
United States
Production: Alive from Off Center, Good Machine, Twin Cities Public
  Television
Producers: Alyce Dissette, Ted Hope, John Ligon, Larry Meistrich, James
  Schamus, Neil V. Sieling
Distribution: Fortissimo Films
Director: Hal Hartley
Screenplay: Hal Hartley
Cinematography: Michael Spiller
Editor: Hal Hartley
Sound: Laurel Bridges, Matthew Price, Reilly Steele
Music: Hal Hartley (as Ned Rifle)
Production Designer: Steven Rosenzweig
Cast: George Feaster, Patricia Sullivan, Rick Groel, Chris Buck, Jim
  McCauley, David Troup, Margaret Mendelson, Julie Sukman, Lasker, Bill
  Sage, Larry Meistrich, Michael McGarry, Casey Finch, Adam Bresnick,
  Elizabeth Feaster, Francie Swift, Lisa Gorlitsky, Mark V. Lake, Bob Gosse,
  Ernesto Gerona, Nancy Kricorian

Color
8 min., 50 sec.
35mm
(Released on the *Surviving Desire* DVD. Wellspring Media, 2002.)

Theory of Achievement (1991)
United States
Production: Alive from Off Center, Yo Productions Ltd. No. 2
Producers: Ted Hope, Larry Meistrich
Distribution: Fortissimo Films
Director: Hal Hartley
Screenplay: Hal Hartley
Cinematography: Michael Spiller
Editor: Hal Hartley
Sound: Jeff Pullman, Tom Paul
Music: Hal Hartley (as Ned Rifle), John Stearns; "Let Me Win Lotto,"
    "Tango" (Jeff Howard); "Die in My Dreams" (Lyrics by Ned Rifle)
Production Designer: Steven Rosenzweig
Cast: Bob Gosse, Jessica Sager, Jeffrey Howard, Bill Sage, Elina Löwensohn,
    Naledi Tshazibane, Nick Gomez, M. C. Bailey, Ingrid Rudefors
Color
17 min., 38 sec.
35mm
(Released on the *Surviving Desire* DVD. Wellspring Media, 2002.)

NYC 3/94 (1994)
United States, Germany
Production: Leapfrog, ZDF, Arte, Open City Films, NYC Postcards
Producers: Chantal Bernheim, Hal Hartley, Ted Hope, Larry Meistrich, Trish
    Sullivan
Distribution: Possible Films
Director: Hal Hartley
Screenplay: Hal Hartley
Cinematography: Hal Hartley, Mark Bailey
Editor: Hal Hartley
Sound: Jeanne Gilliland
Costume Designer: Michelle McDonald
Cast: Dwight Ewell, Liana Pai, Paul Schulze, James Urbaniak
Color
10 min.
Hi-8 Video
(*Possible Films: Short Works by Hal Hartley, 1994–2004*. DVD. Possible
    Films, 2004.)

Opera No. 1 (1994)
United States
Production: Possible Films (2004)
Producers: Jerome Brownstein, Ary Park
Distribution: Possible Films
Director: Hal Hartley
Screenplay: Hal Hartley
Cinematography: Michael Spiller
Editor: Steve Silkensen
Edit and Matchback: Richard Sylvarnes (2004)
Sound: Justin Kawashima (2004)
Music: Hal Hartley; Singers: Lydia Kavanagh, Molly O'Mara, Jeff Howard
Production Designer: Steve Rosenzweig
Costume Designer: Prudence Moriarty
Cast: Patricia Dunnock, Parker Posey, Adrienne Shelly, James Urbaniak
Color
6 min., 54 sec.
35mm
(*Possible Films: Short Works by Hal Hartley, 1994–2004.* DVD. Possible
    Films, 2004.)

The Other Also (1997)
United States, France
Production: Commissioned for Foundation Cartier Pour l'art Contemporain
Distribution: Possible Films
Director: Hal Hartley
Screenplay: Hal Hartley
Cinematography: Hal Hartley
Cast: Elina Löwensohn, Miho Nikaido, with the voice of James Urbaniak
Color
7 min., 18 sec.
Digital Video
(*Possible Films: Short Works by Hal Hartley, 1994–2004.* DVD. Possible
    Films, 2004.)

The New Math(s) (1999)
United States, Great Britain, Netherlands
Production: BBC, NPS Television, True Fiction Pictures, Pipeline Films
Producers: Jerome Brownstein, Susan Leber, Christian Seidel, Rodney
    Wilson, Henk Van Der Meulen
Distribution: Possible Films
Director: Hal Hartley
Screenplay: Hal Hartley

Cinematography: Richard Sylvarnes
Editor: Ben Tudhope
Music: Louis Andriessen, Michel Van Der Aa; Music performed by Ensemble
   Electra
Choreography: David Neumann
Costume Designer: Monica Willis
Make-up: Claus Lulla
Cast: D. J. Mendel, David Neumann, Miho Nikaido
Color
15 min., 6 sec.
Video
(*Possible Films: Short Works by Hal Hartley, 1994–2004.* DVD. Possible
   Films, 2004.)

Kimono (2000)
Production: Ziegler Film, P-Kino Films, True Fiction Pictures
Production: Jerome Brownstein, Thierry Cagignut, Hartmut Koehler, Tanja
   Meding, Matthew Myers, Regina Zeigler
Distribution: Possible Films
Director: Hal Hartley
Screenplay: Hal Hartley
Cinematography: Sarah Cawley
Editor: Steve Silkensen
Music: Hal Hartley
Art Director: Andy Biscontini
Sound: Dave Patterson
Costume Designer: Monica Willis
Make-up: Claus Lulla
Poems: Ono no Komachi (834-?), Izumi Shikibu (974?-1034?); translated by
   Miho Nikaido
Cast: Valerie Cellis (Wood Nymph), Ling (The Ghost), Miho Nikaido (Bride),
   Yun Shen (Wood Nymph)
Color
27 min., 13 sec.
35mm
(*Possible Films: Short Works by Hal Hartley, 1994–2004.* DVD. Possible
   Films, 2004.)

Excerpts from *Soon* (2001)
Production: Possible Films
Producer: Lisa Porter
Distribution: Possible Films
Director: Hal Hartley

Screenplay: Hal Hartley
Editor: Richard Sylvarnes
Music: Hal Hartley, Jim Coleman
Sound: Andy Russ
Cast: Emily Coates, Stacy Dawson, D. J. Mendel, Elina Löwensohn, David
     Neumann, Tom O'Connor, James Stanley
Color
16 min.
Video
(*Possible Films: Short Works by Hal Hartley, 1994–2004*. DVD. Possible
     Films, 2004.)

Sisters of Mercy (2004)
Production: Possible Films
Screenplay: Hal Hartley, Parker Posey, and Sabrina Lloyd
Sound: Justin Kawashima
Cast: Parker Posey, Sabrina Lloyd
Color
16 min., 40 sec.
Hi-8 Video
(*Possible Films: Short Works by Hal Hartley, 1994–2004*. DVD. Possible
     Films, 2004.)

Accomplice (2010)
Production: Possible Films
Distribution: Possible Films
Director: Hal Hartley
Cast: Jordana Maurer, Jean-Luc Godard (archival footage), David Bordwell
     (voice), D.J. Mendel (voice), David Poeppel (voice)
3 min.
(*Possible Films Volume 2: New Short Films by Hal Hartley*. DVD. Possible
     Films, 2010.)

Adventure (2010)
Production: Possible Films
Distribution: Possible Films
Director: Hal Hartley
Editor: Hal Hartley
Cast: Hal Hartley, Miho Nikaido
20 min.
(*Possible Films Volume 2: New Short Films by Hal Hartley*. DVD. Possible
     Films, 2010.)

A/Muse (2010)
Production: Possible Films
Distribution: Possible Films
Director: Hal Hartley
Screenplay: Hal Hartley
Editor: Hal Hartley
Cast: Christina Flick
11 min.
(*Possible Films Volume 2: New Short Films by Hal Hartley*. DVD. Possible
  Films, 2010.)

The Apologies (2010)
Production: Possible Films
Distribution: Possible Films
Director: Hal Hartley
Screenplay: Hal Hartley
Music: Hal Hartley
Cast: Nikolai Kinski, Bettina Zimmermann, Ireen Kirsch
13 min.
(*Possible Films Volume 2: New Short Films by Hal Hartley*. DVD. Possible
  Films, 2010.)

Implied Harmonies (2010)
Production: Possible Films
Production Management: Kyle Gilman
Distribution: Possible Films
Director: Hal Hartley
Cast: Louis Andriessen, Kyle Gilman, Hal Hartley, Jordana Maurer, Claron
  McFadden, Jeroen Willems, Cristina Zavalloni
28 min.
(*Possible Films Volume 2: New Short Films by Hal Hartley*. DVD. Possible
  Films, 2010.)

Accomando, Beth. "Cinema Junkie." *KPBS*, May 17, 2007; accessed June 1, 2010. http://www.kpbs.org/news/2007/may/17/cinema-junkie-by-beth -accomando/.

"Adding Up the Score for the Whole Picture." *Blueprint* 181 (March 2001): 19.

Als, Hilton. "True Stories: The Shock of P. J. Harvey." *New Yorker*, August 20, 2001, 99.

Andersen, Kevin Taylor. "Finding the Essential: A Phenomenological Look at Hal Hartley's *No Such Thing.*" *Film and Philosophy* 7 (2003): 77–91.

Andrew, Geoff. *Stranger Than Paradise: Maverick Film-Makers in Recent American Cinema.* New York: Limelight Editions, 1999.

Andrews, David. "Poking *Henry Fool* with a Stick." *Film Criticism* 24 (1999): 1–21.

Armstrong, Matthew. "Boutiques." *Post Magazine*, February 1, 2005; accessed June 1, 2010. www.postmagazine.com/ME2/dirmod.asp?sid=&nm=&type= Publishing&mod=Publications%3A%3AArticle&mid=8F3A70274218419 78F18BE895F87F791&tier=4&id=AF9E074C962846CD9D0F35126839 F30C.

Atkinson, Michael. "Purchase Power." *Village Voice*, March 9, 1999; accessed June 1, 2010. http://www.villagevoice.com/1999–03–09/film/purchase -power/.

Bauer, Douglas. "An Independent Vision." *Atlantic Monthly* 273.4 (April 1994): 108–14.

Bordwell, David. "Up Close and Impersonal: Hal Hartley and the Persistence of Tradition." *16:9* 3.12 (June 2005); accessed March 14, 2008. http://www.16–9 .dk/2005–06/side11_inenglish.htm.

Bowen, Peter. "What's Love Got to Do with It?" *Filmmaker* (Spring 1995); accessed March 14, 2008. www.filmmakermagazine.com/spring1995/whats_ love.php.

Branigan, Edward. *Narrative Comprehension and Film.* New York: Routledge, 1993.

Bredehoft, Thomas A. "Comics Architecture, Multidimensionality, and Time: Chris Ware's *Jimmy Corrigan: The Smartest Kid on Earth.*" *Modern Fiction Studies* 52.4 (2006): 869–90.

Canby, Vincent. "Mismatched Brothers on a Godardian Road." *New York Times,* October 14, 1992.

Carr, David. "Sundance Dream Most Notable for an Absence." *New York Times,* January 19, 2007.

Chow, Rey. "An Addiction from Which We Never Get Free." *New Literary History* 36 (2005): 47–55.

Clark, John. "Survival Tips for the Aging Independent Filmmaker." *New York Times,* October 1, 2006.

Comer, Brooke. "*Amateur's* Tenebrous Images." *American Cinematographer* 913 (August 1995): 70–74.

Corliss, Richard. "Adding Kick to the Chic." *Time,* November 16, 1992.

———. "Hal Does Have a Heart." *Time,* July 13, 1998.

Corrigan, Timothy. *A Cinema without Walls: Movies and Culture after Vietnam.* New Brunswick, N.J.: Rutgers University Press, 1991.

Craciun, Adriana. "*No Such Thing.*" *Gothic Studies* 5.1 (2003): 129–32.

De Jonge, Peter. "The Jean-Luc Godard of Long Island." *New York Times Magazine,* August 4, 1996, 18–21.

Deer, Lesley. "The Repetition of Difference: Marginality and the Films of Hal Hartley." Ph.D. dissertation, University of Newcastle-upon-Tyne, 2000.

———. "Hal Hartley." In *Fifty Contemporary Filmmakers.* Ed. Yvonne Tasker. New York: Routledge, 2002. 161–69.

Derryberry, Jil. "Have You Seen Elina?" (Interview with Elina Löwensohn). *Interview* 25.4 (April 1995): 32–33.

Donovan, Martin. "Hal Hartley" (Interview). *Bomb* 37 (Fall 1991): 33–35; accessed June 1, 2010. http://bombsite.com/issues/37/articles/1482.

Durbin, Karen. "The Millennium in Perspective, without Hoopla." *New York Times,* March 7, 1999.

Eaves, Hannah. "'Free to Investigate': Hal Hartley." *GreenCine.com,* April 24, 2005; accessed March 13, 2008. https://www.greencine.com/article?action=view&articleID=206.

Ferko, Peter, and Claire Adas. "Interview: Hal Hartley." *Artists Unite.org,* March 10, 2007; accessed March 13, 2008. http://artistsunite-ny.org/blog/?p=943.

Feuer, Jane. "The Self-Reflexive Musical and the Myth of Entertainment." In *Film Genre Reader II.* Ed. Barry Keith Grant. Austin: University of Texas Press, 1995. 441–55.

Fried, John. "Rise of an Indie." *Cineaste* 19.4 (March 1993): 38–40.

Fried, Michael. "Between Realisms: From Derrida to Manet." *Critical Inquiry* 21 (1994): 1–36.

Fuller, Graham. "Being an Amateur." Interview with Hal Hartley. In *Amateur,* by Hal Hartley. London: Faber and Faber, 1994. x–xlix.

———. "Finding the Essential: Hal Hartley in Conversation with Graham Fuller, 1992." In *Hal Hartley: Collected Screenplays 1*, by Hal Hartley. London: Faber and Faber, 2002. vii–xxix.

———. "Hal Hartley: Doing Damage." Introduction to *Amateur*, by Hal Hartley. London: Faber and Faber, 1994. vii–ix.

———. "Indie Film Losing Its Vigor as It Ages." *New York Times*, May 2, 1999.

———. "Responding to Nature: Hal Hartley in Conversation with Graham Fuller." In *Henry Fool*, by Hal Hartley. London: Faber and Faber, 1998. vii–xxv.

Gates, Anita. "Feeling a Link to the Spiritual Unknown." *New York Times*, September 29, 2004.

Gewertz, Ken. "Independent Eye: Filmmaker Hal Hartley Sees Things His Own Way." *Harvard University Gazette*, March 21, 2002; accessed June 1, 2010. http://www.news.harvard.edu/gazette/2002/03.21/09-hartley.html.

Gilbey, Ryan. "Pulling the Pin on Hal Hartley." In *American Independent Cinema: A Sight and Sound Reader*. Ed. Jim Hillier. London: British Film Institute, 2001. 142–45.

———. "Reheating Hal Hartley." *The Guardian*, March 9, 2007; accessed June 1, 2010. www.guardian.co.uk/film/2007/mar/09/2.

Gunning, Tom. "Thrice upon a Time: Flirting with a Film by Hal Hartley." Preface to *Flirt*, by Hal Hartley. London: Faber and Faber, 1996. vii–x.

"Hal Hartley: The Last Auteur." Directors in Focus Series. Harvard Film Archive (January–February 2001); accessed March 13, 2008. http://hcl.harvard.edu/hfa/films/2001janfeb/hartley.html.

Hansen, Miriam. "'With Skin and Hair': Kracauer's Theory of Film, Marseilles 1940." *Critical Inquiry* 19 (1993): 437–69.

Harmetz, Aljean. "Big and Little Buzzes at the Sundance Festival." *New York Times*, January 24, 1991.

Hartley, Hal. "Actually Responding." Introduction to *Flirt*, by Hal Hartley. London: Faber and Faber, 1996. xi–xix.

———. "Adventure: A Screenplay by Hal Hartley Composed of E-Mail Messages Received from Douglas Gordon, December 1998." In *Douglas Gordon: Through a Looking Glass*. New York: Gagosian Gallery, 1999. N.p.

———. *Amateur*. London: Faber and Faber, 1994.

———. "The Director Interview: Hal Hartley, *Fay Grim*." *Filmmaker*, May 18, 2007; accessed March 12, 2008. http://filmmakermagazine.com/directorinterviews/2007/05/hal-hartley-fay-grim.html.

———. "Flirt." In *Projections 3: Film-makers on Film-making*. Ed. John Boorman and Walter Donohue. London: Faber and Faber, 1994. 262–80.

———. *Flirt*. London: Faber and Faber, 1996.

———. *Hal Hartley: Collected Screenplays 1*. London: Faber and Faber, 2002.

———. *Henry Fool*. London: Faber and Faber, 1998.

——. "indieWIRE Interview: *Fay Grim* Director Hal Hartley." *indieWIRE*, May 14, 2007; accessed May 17, 2010. http://www.indiewire.com/article/indiewire_interview_fay_grim_director_hal_hartley/.

——. "In Images We Trust: Hal Hartley Chats with Jean-Luc Godard." *Filmmaker* (Fall 1994): 14–18, 55–56.

——. "Interview with Hal Hartley." *Los Angeles Journal*, July 10, 2007; accessed March 13, 2008. http://www.losangelesjournal.com/new/articles-view -3–417.

——. "Knowing Is Not Enough." In *Projections: Film-makers on Film-making*. Ed. John Boorman and Walter Donohue. London: Faber and Faber, 1992. 223.

——. *Possible Films: Short Works by Hal Hartley, 1994–2004*. DVD. Possible Films, 2004.

——. "Surviving Desire." In *Projections: Film-makers on Film-making*. Ed. John Boorman and Walter Donohue. London: Faber and Faber, 1992. 224–59.

Hartley, Hal, and Kenneth Kaleta. *True Fiction Pictures and Possible Films: Hal Hartley in Conversation with Kenneth Kaleta*. New York: Soft Skull Press, 2008.

"Hartley, Hal." *Current Biography*. 56th ed. New York: H. W. Wilson, 1995. 235–38.

Harvey, Sylvia. *May '68 and Film Culture*. London: British Film Institute, 1980.

Hauser, Christine, and Al Baker. "Keeping Wary Eye on Crime as Economy Sinks." *New York Times*, October 9, 2008.

Hernandez, Eugene. "Digital Video: Catch the Wave." *Independent Film and Video Monthly* 22 (January–February 1999): 30–32.

——. "Hal Hartley Takes Latest Film to Netflix for DVD Release." *indieWIRE*, July 6, 2005; accessed June 1, 2010. http://www.indiewire.com/article/hal_hartley_takes_latest_film_to_netflix_for_dvd_release/.

——. "Possible Films Unveils *Unknowing*, Plans More Films in Theaters and on DVD." *indieWIRE*, September 29, 2004; accessed June 1, 2010. http://www.indiewire.com/article/possible_films_unveils_unknowing_plans_more_films_in_theaters_and_on_dvd/.

Hernandez, Eugene, and Brian Brooks. "Toronto '06 Daily Dispatch: Hal Hartley Back with *Fay Grim;* Eytan Fox's Latest, *The Bubble*." *indieWIRE*, September 14, 2006; accessed June 1, 2010. http://www.indiewire.com/article/toronto_06_daily_dispatch_hal_hartley_back_with_fay_grim_eytan_fox_latest_t/.

Hershenson, Roberta. "Young Acting Program Comes of Age." *New York Times*, February 28, 1993.

Hevesi, Dennis. "Adrienne Shelly, 40, an Actress, Film Director and Screenwriter." *New York Times*, November 4, 2006.

Higher Definition with Robert Wilonsky. Prod. Michelle Mesenbrink. On *Fay Grim* DVD. Magnolia Home Entertainment, 2007.

Hill, Logan. "Resident Alien: Whatever Happened to Hal Hartley?" *New York,* May 21, 2005, 71.

Hillier, Jim, ed. *American Independent Cinema: A* Sight and Sound *Reader.* London: British Film Institute, 2001.

Hoberman, J. "Dirt Cheap." *Village Voice,* June 23, 1998, 135.

Hogue, Peter. "Band of Outsiders." *Film Comment* 29.1 (January–February 1993): 69–71.

Holden, Stephen. "Battling Evildoers from Worldwide Headquarters in Woodside, Queens." *New York Times,* May 18, 2007.

———. "Looking for Love in Three Different Places." *New York Times,* October 6, 1995.

———. "The Millennium in Fable and Reality." *New York Times,* October 10, 1998.

———. "Party On! It's a Civic Duty." *New York Times,* May 4, 2005.

Hollinger, Karen. "Film Noir, Voice-Over, and the Femme Fatale." In *Film Noir Reader.* Ed. Alain Silver and James Ursini. New York: Limelight Editions, 1996. 243–59.

"Hollywood's Kindergarten (American Independent Filmmakers)." *The Economist,* February 26, 1994, 89–90.

Holmlund, Chris, and Justin Wyatt, eds. *Contemporary American Independent Film: From the Margins to the Mainstream.* New York: Routledge, 2005.

Hope, Ted. "Back to the Future." *New York Times,* January 18, 2005.

James, Caryn. "Applying 1950's Cool to the 80's." *New York Times,* July 20, 1990.

———. "Critic's Choice: A Survey of Films by Hartley." *New York Times,* January 13, 1995.

———. "Critic's Notebook: Hollywood Tactics Invade the Sundance Festival." *New York Times,* February 5, 1990.

———. "Film View: This Director's Characters Have an Attitude." *New York Times,* November 1, 1992.

———. "The Nun, the Amnesiac, the Prostitute and the Thugs." *New York Times,* September 29, 1994.

———. "*Trust:* Black Humor and Unlikely Lovers." *New York Times,* July 26, 1991.

Jameson, Fredric. *Brecht and Method.* London: Verso, 1998.

———. *Signatures of the Visible.* New York: Routledge, 1990.

Jones, Kent. "Hal Hartley: The Book I Read Was in Your Eyes." *Film Comment* 32.4 (July–August 1996): 68–72.

Kaufman, Anthony. "Ghost of the Machine." *Village Voice,* June 4, 2002.

———. "Hal Fool: The Push, Pull and Play of Hal Hartley, Part I." *indieWIRE,*

June 18, 1998; accessed June 1, 2010. http://www.indiewire.com/article/hal_
fool_the_push_pull_and_play_of_hal_hartley_part_i/.

———. "Hal Fool: The Push, Pull and Play of Hal Hartley, Part II." *indieWIRE*,
June 19, 1998; accessed June 1, 2010. http://www.indiewire.com/article/hal_
fool_the_push_pull_and_play_of_hal_hartley_part_ii/.

———. "Has Indie Slipped Its Hip?" *Daily Variety*, September 7, 2005.

———. "Monsters, Media and Meaning: Hal Hartley on *No Such Thing*." *indieWIRE*, March 26, 2002; accessed June 1, 2010. http://www.indiewire.com/
article/interview_monsters_media_and_meaning_hal_hartley_on_no_such_
thing/.

Kauffmann, Stanley. "Billionaires and Lesser Folk." *New Republic*, September
2, 1991, 26–27.

———. "A Mystery, a Romance." *New Republic*, July 13, 1998, 26–27.

———. "Viewing the Past." *New Republic*, April 25, 1995, 30–31.

Kehr, Dave. "At the Movies." *New York Times*, March 29, 2002.

King, Geoff. *American Independent Cinema*. Bloomington: Indiana University
Press, 2005.

Kipp, Jeremiah. "The Tao of Steve" (Interview with Steve Hamilton). *Movie-
Maker*, February 3, 2007; accessed June 1, 2010. http://www.moviemaker
.com/editing/article/the_tao_of_steve_2785/.

Klein, Alvin. "Emerging from an Unhappy Childhood on L.I." (Interview with
Adrienne Shelley). *New York Times*, July 28, 1991.

Krämer, Peter. *The New Hollywood: From* Bonnie and Clyde *to* Star Wars.
London: Wallflower Press, 2005.

Levy, Ellen. "Hal Hartley's Moments of Truth." *Independent* 15 (October 1992):
22–27.

Levy, Emanuel. *Cinema of Outsiders: The Rise of American Independent Film*.
New York: New York University Press, 1999.

Lewis, Jon, ed. *The New American Cinema*. Durham, N.C.: Duke University
Press, 1998.

Lyon, Donald. *Independent Visions: A Critical Introduction to Recent Independent American Film*. New York: Ballantine Books, 1994.

MacCabe, Colin. "Realism and the Cinema." In *Tracking the Signifier: Theoretical Essays on Film, Linguistics, Literature*. Minneapolis: University of
Minnesota Press, 1985. 33–57.

———. "Theory and Film: Principles of Realism and Pleasure." In *Tracking the
Signifier: Theoretical Essays on Film, Linguistics, Literature*. Minneapolis:
University of Minnesota Press, 1985. 58–81.

The Making of Fay Grim; or, How Do You Spell Espionage? Prod. Kyle Gilman.
Fay Grim DVD. Magnolia Home Entertainment, 2007.

Man, Glenn. *Radical Visions: American Film Renaissance, 1967–1976*. Westport,
Conn.: Greenwood Press, 1994.

Margulies, Ivone, ed. *Rites of Realism: Essays on Corporeal Cinema*. Durham, N.C.: Duke University Press, 2003.

Maslin, Janet. "The Calm Instead of the Storm at Cannes." *New York Times,* May 21, 1998.

———. "Critic's Notebook: At Cannes, Tim Robbins Proves a Double Threat." *New York Times,* May 13, 1992.

———. "Of Faustian Wonders and a Mythic Queens." *New York Times,* June 19, 1998.

———. "The Two Hollywoods: Meeting Halfway." *New York Times,* November 16, 1997.

"Michael Spiller." *Internet Encyclopedia of Cinematographers,* March 3, 2008; accessed March 13, 2008. http://www.cinematographers.nl/PaginasDoPh/ spiller.htm.

Mitchell, Elvis. "Yes, Someone for Everyone, Even Someone with Fangs." *New York Times,* March 29, 2002.

Morfoot, Addie. "AFI Fest/Ten Cinematographers to Watch." *Daily Variety,* November 2, 2006.

Murphy, J. J. *Me and You and* Memento *and* Fargo: *How Independent Screenplays Work.* New York: Continuum, 2007.

Neale, Steve, and Murray Smith, eds. *Contemporary Hollywood Cinema.* New York: Routledge, 1998.

Nicklas, Jens. "Parody, Poetry, and the Periphery: Hal Hartley's *Amateur." Film Journal* 1.5 (May 2003); accessed April 18, 2007. http://www.thefilmjournal .com/issue5/amateur.html.

Ochiva, Dan. "Top Producers: Hal Hartley." *Millimeter* 19 (January 1991): 91.

O'Connor, John J. "Some Loners Struggle with Love and Survival." *New York Times,* January 22, 1992.

Pall, Ellen. "The Elusive Women Who Inhabit the Quirky Films of Hal Hartley." *New York Times,* April 9, 1995.

———. "This Director's Wish List Doesn't Include Hollywood" (Interview with Hal Hartley). *New York Times,* October 11, 1992.

Phillips, Sarah. "A 'Breakthrough' Film?" *CineAction!* 47 (September 1998): 45–47.

Pride, Ray. "Reversal of Fortune." *Filmmaker* (Summer 1998); accessed June 2, 2010. http://www.filmmakermagazine.com/issues/summer1998/fortune .php.

Professional Amateurs: The Making of Amateur. On *Amateur* DVD. Sony Pictures Classics / Columbia Tristar Home Entertainment, 2003.

Rabin, Nathan. Rev. of *Fay Grim. A.V. Club,* May 17, 2007; accessed June 2, 2010. http://www.avclub.com/articles/fay-grim,3464/.

Remila, Laurence. "Godard's Sons: Why Are They All Bastards?" *Vertigo* 1 (1997): 21–23.

Rodowick, D. N. *The Crisis of Political Modernism: Criticism and Ideology in Contemporary Film Theory.* 2d ed. Berkeley: University of California Press, 1994.

Ross, Matthew. "Separation Anxiety? Not for Ex–Good Machiners at 'This Is That.'" *indieWIRE,* September 24, 2002; accessed June 2, 2010. http://www.indiewire.com/article/interview_separation_anxiety_not_for_ex-good_machiners_at_this_is_that/.

Rowe, Claudia. "Film Makers Take Root at Purchase." *New York Times,* November 2, 1997.

Sánchez, Sergi. *Las Variaciones Hartley; entrevista de Kenneth Kaleta* (The Hartley variations; Interview with Kenneth Kaleta). Gijón, Spain: Festival Internacional de Cine de Gijón, 2003.

Sarris, Andrew. "The Care and Feeding of Auteurs: Trusting Hal Hartley." *Film Comment* 29.1 (January–February 1993): 66–68.

Schoemer, Karen. "New Faces: Adrienne Shelley and Robert Burke, Two Performers Who've Lived Their Roles." *New York Times,* July 27, 1990.

Sconce, Jeffrey. "Irony, Nihilism, and the New American 'Smart' Film." *Screen* 43 (2002): 349–69.

Shary, Timothy. *Generation Multiplex: The Image of Youth in Contemporary American Cinema.* Austin: University of Texas Press, 2002.

Smith, Gavin. "'People Like to Say, "What Do You Mean Exactly?" I Would Answer, "I Mean, but Not Exactly"': Jean-Luc Godard Interviewed by Gavin Smith." *Film Comment* 32.4 (March–April 1996): 31–41.

Sobchack, Vivian. "Lounge Time: Postwar Crises and the Chronotope of Film Noir." In *Refiguring American Film Genres: History and Theory.* Ed. Nick Browne. Berkeley: University of California Press, 1998. 129–70.

Sobczynsk, Peter. "An Interview with Hal Hartley." *24fps,* n.d.; accessed March 13, 2008. http://www.24fpsmagazine.com/Archive/Hartley.html.

Sonnet, Esther. "Desire and Delusion: *Amateur* and Postmodern Heterosexuality." In *Just Postmodernism.* Ed. Steven Earnshaw. Amsterdam: Rodopi, 1997. 261–77.

"Special Indie Section." *DGA Magazine* 27.5 (January 2003): 44–84.

Stern, Lesley. "Paths That Wind through the Thickets of Things." *Critical Inquiry* 28 (2001): 315–54.

Stern, Lesley, and George Kouvaros. "Descriptive Acts." Introduction to *Falling for You: Essays on Cinema and Performance.* Ed. Lesley Stern and George Kouvaros. Urbana: University of Illinois Press, 1999. 1–35.

Sterritt, David. "A Filmmaker's Take on the Nature of Identity." *Christian Science Monitor* April 5, 1995, 12.

Suárez, Juan A. *Jim Jarmusch.* Urbana: University of Illinois Press, 2007.

Thomson, Patricia. "A Futuristic Farce in Manhattan." *American Cinematographer* 86.3 (March 2005): 99–100.

Timberg, Scott. "American Nowhere: Hal Hartley on Realism, Surrealism, and

Henry Fool." *SF Weekly,* July 8, 1998; accessed March 13, 2008. http://search .sfweekly.com/1998-07-08/film/american-nowhere/.

Tobias, Scott. Interview with Hal Hartley. *A.V. Club,* April 3, 2002; accessed March 13, 2008. http://www.avclub.com/content/node/22663.

Tommasini, Anthony. "A Hip Audience Packs the Hall to Hear Hip Works." *New York Times,* October 3, 2000.

"Twenty-five Years of the Sundance Institute." *Filmmaker* 15.1 (Fall 2006): 57–89.

Tzioumakis, Yannis. *American Independent Cinema.* New Brunswick, N.J.: Rutgers University Press, 2006.

Upon Reflection: Trust. Prod. Kyle Gilman. On *Trust* DVD. Aztec International, the AV Channel, 1999.

Weber, Bruce. "Big Movies on Little Budgets." *New York Times,* May 17, 1992.

Winters, Laura. "For an Art-House Regular, a Wider World" (Interview with Martin Donovan). *New York Times,* April 13, 1997.

Wise, Sophie. "What I Like about Hal Hartley, or Rather, What Hal Hartley Likes about Me: The Performance of the (Spect)actor." In *Falling For You: Essays on Cinema and Performance.* Ed. Lesley Stern and George Kouvaros. Urbana: University of Illinois Press, 1999. 245–75.

Wood, David. "Career Profile: Hal Hartley." *BBC.* Accessed March 12, 2008. http://www.bbc.co.uk/films/2001/03/15/hal_hartley_career_profile_article .shtml.

Wood, Jason. Interview with Hal Hartley. In *Talking Movies: Contemporary World Filmmakers in Interview.* London: Wallflower Press, 2006. 103–15.

———. *The Pocket Essentials: Hal Hartley.* Harpenden, U.K.: Pocket Essentials, 2003.

92–94; and religion, 4, 24; and saintly women in films, 25, 34–35; and Simone Weil script, 85–86; and social scrutiny and surveillance in films, 1, 8–10, 15, 25, 33–34, 63, 68; and stages of career and retrospectives, 8, 33–34, 68, 83–84; and True Fiction Pictures (production company), 76; and use of titles, intertitles, and credits, 9, 16, 39, 44, 49, 53–56. *See also individual films*
Harvard University, 8, 87
Harvey, P. J., 57, 59, 62, 66
Hauser, Christine, 34
Hayes, Isaac, 62
Haynes, Todd, 7, 76
Healy, David, 10
Henry Fool, 41–49, 77, 83; and award at Cannes film festival, 8; and budget, 75; and cinematography, 53; and conclusion, 48–49, 52, 88; and dark tone, 71; and mourning, 42; and music, 90–91; and pornography, 43–45, 47; and published screenplay, 49; and scope of narrative, 56, 72–74, 76, 87–90
Heteronormativity, 4–5, 14–15
Heys, J. E., 51
Higher Definition with Robert Wilonsky, 41–42, 49, 61
Hillier, Jim, 69n5
Hollinger, Karen, 62
Holmlund, Chris, 69n5
Hope, Ted, 6
Howard, Jeffrey, 23
Hunt, Marko, 16
Huppert, Isabelle, 25, 34–35

"indieWIRE interview," 69n5
"Interview with Hal Hartley" (Los Angeles Journal), 69n1

James, Caryn, 9, 11, 27
Jameson, Fredric, 2–3, 54
Jarmusch, Jim, 3–4, 7, 40, 69n3, 69n5

Kaleta, Kenneth, 5, 69n1, 69n5
Karina, Anna, 31–32
Kaufmann, Stanley, 19
Kimono, 70n13

King, Geoff, 69n5
Kinski, Nikolai, 70n12
"Kool Thing" (Sonic Youth), 28, 31
Koteas, Elias, 78

Lanko, Vivian, 24–25
Lee, Ang, 7
Lee, Spike, 7
Levy, Emanuel, 69n5
Lewis, Jon, 69n5
Lindenhurst, Long Island, 5, 9, 13, 23–24
"Love Too Soon" (Pascal Comelade and P. J. Harvey), 59
Löwensohn, Elina, 7, 25, 30–31, 35, 51
Luddy, Tom, 93
Lulu, 66

MacCabe, Colin, 2–3
MacKay, John, 7, 17, 23
MacMurray, Fred, 41
Mad Judy Productions, 6
Madonna, 27, 32
Making of Fay Grim; or How Do You Spell Espionage? The, 69n7
Malick, Terrence, 10, 75, 78–79
Malloy, Matt, 7, 16–17, 24–25
Man, Glenn, 69n5
Maral, Adnan, 70n11
Marich, Marietta, 23
Massachusetts College of Art, 5
Mayfield, Katherine, 10
McKenzie, Mary, 23, 34
McNeal, Julia, 10
Meek, Donald, 69n6
Mendel, D. J., 7, 49, 58
Miéville, Anne-Marie, 84
Mitchell, Thomas, 69n6
Montgomery, Chuck, 7, 36, 41

Nashville, 82
Nebbou, Mehdi, 55
Nelson, Rebecca Merritt, 7, 16
New World, The, 78
Nikaido, Miho, 7–8, 46, 59, 83–84, 86
Nolte, Nick, 78
No Such Thing, 6, 25, 57, 79; and cinematography, 83; and genre, 92; and music, 90; and onscreen microphones, 63

Mark L. Berrettini is an assistant professor of
film studies in the department of theater arts
at Portland State University, where he teaches
in film history, theory, genre, and screenwriting.

The University of Illinois Press
is a founding member of the
Association of American University Presses.

Composed in 10/13 New Caledonia LT Std
with Helvetica Neue display
by Celia Shapland
at the University of Illinois Press
Manufactured by Cushing-Malloy, Inc.

University of Illinois Press
1325 South Oak Street
Champaign, IL 61820-6903
www.press.uillinois.edu